THE BREAKING POINT

THE
BREAKING
POINT

How Today's Women Are
Navigating Midlife Crisis

◆ ◆ ◆

Sue Shellenbarger

An Owl Book

Henry Holt and Company · New York

Owl Books
Henry Holt and Company, LLC
Publishers since 1866
175 Fifth Avenue
New York, New York 10010
www.henryholt.com

An Owl Book® and 🏛® are registered trademarks
of Henry Holt and Company, LLC.

Distributed in Canada by H. B. Fenn and Company Ltd.

Library of Congress Cataloging-in-Publication Data
Shellenbarger, Sue.
The breaking point : how today's women are navigating midlife crisis /
Sue Shellenbarger.—1st ed.
p.   cm.
Includes bibliographical references.
ISBN-13: 978-0-8050-8031-5
ISBN-10: 0-8050-8031-7
1. Middle aged women—Psychology.   2. Middle aged women—Attitudes.
3. Middle aged women—Conduct of life.   4. Midlife crisis.   I. Title.
HQ1059.4.S46   2005
305.24'2—dc22

Henry Holt books are available for special promotions
and premiums. For details contact: Director, Special Markets.

Originally published in hardcover in 2005 by Henry Holt

First Owl Books Edition 2005

Designed by Victoria Hartman

Printed in the United States of America

1   3   5   7   9   10   8   6   4   2

To my children:
Margaret, Rich, Lucas,
Cristin, and James

✦

Contents

✦ ✦ ✦

Introduction

✦　✦　✦

Careening down a mountain on an all-terrain vehicle, I struggle for control as my ATV bounces off ruts and roots. A teenage friend leading the way on his dirt bike waves his hand in a "Slow down!" signal.

I ignore him. At 51, I am hell-bent on adventure.

Grazing the trunk of a Douglas fir big enough to halt a speeding Humvee, I make a turn on two wheels and hit the throttle. I am invincible. Ageless. Mindless, I might add, of the fact that with scant experience on mountainous terrain, I am like a grenade with the pin pulled, moments from certain disaster.

For twenty-five years, I have been a working mother, juggling home, family, kids, job, and suburban community life with intensity. In middle age, I have become somebody no one knows, a wild woman with graying hair under a full-face helmet, a hand too heavy on the throttle and an adventure lust so consuming that I lie awake nights.

Camping in Oregon's Coastal Range with a hard-riding crowd of off-road adventurers, I am flattered to be invited to join three of the biggest daredevils on the trail. As I gain speed, exhilaration renders gas fumes sweet in my lungs. The trees fly by in a blur, the roar of my engine fills the air. Speed rivets my senses on the moment. I lean into a sharp turn.

Then, in a heartbeat, the ground heaves upward, earthquake-like. A berm erupts and lifts my two right tires. My ATV bucks and starts to roll. Reflexively, I hit the throttle. The earth tilts. My body flies off the seat. Deep-green treetops spin crazily.

My back slams hard onto the dusty red clay of the trail. The sky goes dark as the 375-pound Honda 400EX flips and lands sideways the full length of my body.

When I regain consciousness, three pairs of eyes behind full-face helmets circle the sky overhead, peering down at me like curious aliens landed to search for signs of life. "Can you breathe?" asks one. "Can you move?" comes another voice from beneath a fiberglass face shield.

I move my neck slightly, then my spine, and say a prayer of thanks that I am not paralyzed. "She has the balls of a gorilla, doesn't she?" murmurs one of my companions, thinking I cannot hear.

Their quick-witted rush to hoist the ATV off my body saved me from a worse fate, I later learn. The damage: a collarbone knocked so far out of whack that it looks like some demon battling to escape my skin. A bruise the shape of an ATV extends the length of my torso. I creep painfully onto the back of a friend's ATV and we ride back to camp. My worried children, 12 and 15, and the rest of our campmates circle me, marveling that a collarbone could go so far AWOL, and my friend shuttles me to the nearest emergency room forty miles away.

What was I thinking?

The answer, of course, is that I wasn't thinking. I was only feeling. I had plunged deep into the dark comedy of a midlife crisis.

A series of losses in middle age had left me reeling—the death of my father, the end of my twenty-year marriage in divorce, and the approach of the empty nest as my children grew more independent. Values that had helped guide my life for decades—achievement, frugality, respectability, career success, exceeding other people's expectations—did not matter to me anymore. Beset by an emotional deadness, I felt the truth of Joseph Campbell's quote, "Midlife is when you reach the top of the ladder and find that it was against the wrong wall." For a time, it seemed, repressing my deepest dreams and desires—for adventure, for a simpler, more rustic life, and for closeness with nature and with other people who valued it, too—was no longer worth the sacrifice.

Like most people, I had never taken the notion of midlife crisis seriously. I thought of it as a fleeting, laughable period of adolescent regression that leads middle-aged men to buy red sports cars and take trophy wives. Typing with my arm in a sling after the ATV accident, I attempted to make light of the subject in my "Work & Family" column in *The Wall Street Journal*. Lampooning myself for having one of the stupidest accidents of my life, I wrote, "The midlife crisis is a cliché—until you have one."

I quickly learned I was not alone. The column drew one of the biggest reader responses I had received in twelve years as a columnist. While some readers of both sexes were startled by the notion that a female could even have a midlife crisis ("I had no idea that women got this, too," wrote a Texas man), a far larger number of women readers experienced a shock of self-recognition. Dozens told heartfelt tales of pain, upheaval, rebirth, and transformation in middle age, and said they had no idea other women were experiencing the same thing. My comic tale had touched a hidden nerve. Clearly, millions of midlife women had reached a crisis stage—a time when old values and goals no longer made sense to them.

I began gathering more stories. Through newspaper ads, networking, and e-mail, I identified fifty women who had undergone midlife turmoil, each of whom generously agreed to share her life experience. In thirty years as a journalist, I have not experienced interviews as moving as these. Many agreed to talk for an hour, then went on for four or five. Some shared their artwork, their writings, photos of their gardens, their children, their dogs. Powerful themes of frustration or despair, the resurgence of unsettling passions and desires, self-discovery, and renewal ran through all their stories. From each one, I learned much about the gifts and challenges of midlife.

Shedding Old Selves. Not all women in midlife transition experience such explosive feelings—or bouts of foolishness—as I. There are many paths through this turbulent time. Many women remain calmer and wiser, taking stock of renascent dreams and desires, expressing them in new pursuits and integrating them into their lives. While they undergo a profound change in life direction, these women make changes more smoothly. Others spend a lot of energy repressing midlife desires, only to learn, too late, that stifled dreams have turned to bile in their souls.

Nevertheless, there is a common thread: In all cases, midlife crisis brings traits, needs, or desires that have been ignored or repressed roaring back on center stage in one's personality. We strive at midlife to integrate the pieces of ourselves that we have been missing—to become whole. In the process, we pass two of life's most important milestones, according to psychoanalyst Murray Stein, who has written extensively on midlife: We gain a new understanding of our limits. And we develop a new sense of meaning and direction to guide us through the rest of our lives.[1]

These themes bind together all the stories in my fifty-woman study. A California saleswoman wrote that, at age 50, she was overcome by such a powerful yearning for the intimate love she had never known that she could not bear to watch romantic scenes on TV or in the movies. She soon plunged headlong into the most passionate and transformative love affair of her life, learning for the first time to be truly close to a lover.

Struck at age 48 by a powerful recognition that she had not

been true to herself, or "authentic," in her choices, a midwestern homemaker and community volunteer ended her marriage and poured everything she had into a long-standing dream of founding her own company. Soon, she was CEO of her own successful consulting firm, expressing her vision and talents in the world at large.

A San Francisco consultant quit her business after the long illness and death of her partner of twenty-two years. Then, after a time of grieving, she joined a motorcycle club, had a wild transcontinental love affair, finished law school, and met and married a new husband—all after the age of 41.

Like me, all the women who wrote in response to my column believed they were alone in their struggle. "Thanks for giving me a name for it," wrote a California woman who nearly killed herself at age 40 in a biking accident on the beach. Her midlife transition led her to realize a dream of writing screenplays.

Similar in power to toddlerhood and the teenage years, midlife crisis drives people to shed old selves like a snakeskin. A New York bed-and-breakfast proprietor decides at 50 that life is no longer worth living if she cannot make the artwork she is yearning to create, so she shutters the B&B, ends her marriage, and takes up a career as an artist and art teacher. A 40-year-old homemaker with a lifelong desire to find a spiritual teacher decides after a divorce to make it her top priority, then plunges into a period of such intense personal growth that she winds up as CEO of a fast-growing company. A 43-year-old public-company executive from Colorado quits her job after a divorce, pilots a sailboat across the Mediterranean with a handsome new

French lover, then decides to fulfill a long-standing desire to nurture others by training for a career as a counselor.

"Everyone thought I had lost my mind," she admits.

All this from women with staid past lives and mainstream résumés who, based on the dictates of our culture, should be peacefully adrift by now on the placid seas of middle age.

Such growth comes at a cost. Midlife crisis can be painful and destructive, not only to women but to their loved ones. It can bring "a breathtaking degree of illusion and self-deception," Stein writes, sparking behavior that seems out of character to others, laughable, or simply bizarre. As one woman wrote in an e-mail, "The brooding that turning 50 can trigger makes for a volatile emotional cocktail."

I have been breathing the vapors of that cocktail myself for quite some time. Regaining one's balance during midlife crisis can take years. Four years into my own, I am still neck-deep in change—high on personal growth, as described in new research on middle age reported in this book, but strained in other ways. I did not know it at the time, but I had some hard inner work to do when my midlife crisis erupted at age 49. I needed to pick up and reintegrate some old passions that I had cast aside in my twenties: a love of nature and outdoor adventures. As a Michigan farm kid and an inveterate camper in my teens and twenties, I had dreamed of making my adult life on a farm or in the forest, and of marrying a logger, rancher, or farmer.

I put all that aside in my twenties, left the farm for the city, and set out on the only path I could see toward forging a strong personal identity—investing in a career. I built my life's work in journalism and met and married a good man, an educator and executive reared in the suburbs. Working, helping raise my three beloved stepchildren, and caring for the two birth children who became the center of my life, kept me very, very busy for years. I was the consummate juggler, subsumed by a time-starved workaday routine of job, family, sleep, job, family, sleep. I had no energy left, mental or physical, to imagine anything else.

But as I approached my sixth decade, the losses were mounting. My marriage had fallen victim partly to the strain of our juggling act; my husband and I had neglected old problems so long that they hardened into permanent scars. My father died suddenly after a massive stroke. An empty nest loomed as my two birth children moved deeper into their teens. I felt despair all the time—except when I escaped into the outdoors or new adventures. In a departure from the frugal, staid soccer-mom ways of my past, I started spending money recklessly on sports outings, motorcycle-riding courses, vacations. I played hooky too often from a job I loved, escaping to the only places I could find peace—the forest, the desert, or speeding down a mountain on skis or an ATV.

My midlife crisis peaked when I was 51, when, had anyone been keeping track, the hours I spent racing around in the woods, riding the Oregon dunes, camping, skiing, dancing, and having adventures rivaled those I spent tending to business— writing my column and taking care of my kids and my home. Family and friends shook their heads. My neighborhood homeowner's association asked me to please, clean up my yard. Sometimes, I barely recognized myself. After marching for so long to the drumbeat of work and family, I felt as if I was dancing to some deranged inner bongo-player no one else could hear.

After two bone-crushing ATV crashes, my editor suggested I hire a driver, and my doctor took to asking for Evel Knievel when he called. "I had to check your chart again, to make sure you were fifty-one and not seventeen," he joked. I began seeing a counselor for help reining in my own rebellion. At one point, I lamented to her, "I wish I had gotten this out of my system when I was seventeen."

Today, at 53, I am sobering up from the vapors of midlife ferment. That I have achieved one of the goals of midlife crisis—finding and understanding my limits—is clear every time I look in the mirror. My dislocated collarbone remains so bizarre-looking that my teenage son invites his friends over to see it. After forty-five minutes of pounding and pushing on my shoulder to ram it back into place, my orthopedist and his assistant gave up and declared, not very convincingly, "Don't worry. It doesn't show that much." Shopping for evening and swim wear has become a daunting challenge; turtleneck evening gowns are hard to find.

One task posed by midlife crisis is to act upon what it signifies—that repressing creative, productive, or expressive parts of yourself comes with a cost, and that you must either integrate those facets into your life or come to peace with the fact that you cannot. To that end, I am trying to refashion a more responsible and integrated life, one that not only helps me, my kids, and my friends and neighbors, but that serves as a worthwhile example to others. In so doing, I have also made progress on the second goal of midlife crisis: discovering new meaning in life. I am by no means nearing some late-life nirvana, but I am at least asking more of the right questions.

Ripe for Upheaval. As a society, we greatly underestimate the degree to which we are still developing, growing, and changing at 40 and beyond. Few women are prepared for the explosive desires that can erupt during this life stage. Even fewer are equipped with the knowledge they need to navigate these stormy seas with wisdom.

As a generation, the 42 million–woman baby boom is ripe for upheaval: After decades of juggling careers, the consuming demands of work, child care, elder care, housework, and marriages rendered numb by dual-earner overload—many women of this generation are weary of repressing the parts of themselves they set aside to keep all those balls in the air. Much is at stake: As life spans lengthen, midlife no longer ushers in a decrepit old age or imminent death. Instead, it marks the threshold of what is potentially an entire one-third or even one-half of one's life. The quality of that final phase depends in large part on how well people navigate midlife transitions.

Part I of this book maps a broad trend toward female midlife crisis. In chapter 1, the research of the Gallup Organization, Yankelovich Partners, Leisure Trends, AARP, DDB Worldwide, and other leading sources helps show how female midlife crisis is shaping our culture. Chapter 2 describes the roots of its tremendous psychological power.

Part II of the book provides a new organizing principle for

women in midlife crisis. It documents the six archetypes of midlife crisis that emerged in the life stories of the fifty women who participated in my study: the Adventurer, the Lover, the Leader, the Artist, the Gardener, and the Seeker. Each reflects a set of desires or goals a woman might express or strive for at midlife. Any woman in midlife turmoil should be able to find her driving force here.

Part III distills the meaning of our midlife crises, for each other and for future generations. Chapter 9 shows how midlife crisis shapes well-being in old age and shows ways of sharing the wisdom gained at midlife, through storytelling and women's groups. The final chapter looks at how midlife crisis serves to prepare us for one of life's highest callings: creating a better world for our children and the generations beyond.

Research psychologists and social scientists have long puzzled over why the notion of midlife crisis holds such power in people's minds. Social scientist Elaine Wethington, whose research is documented in chapter 1, attributes its potency to its "symbolism to Americans of the hidden potential of their aging to threaten control over their lives."

To me, its power derives from a deeper source: the surprising discovery that, at midlife, much of life still remains to be lived, that the vital juices of joy, sexuality, and self-discovery are bubbling within, more powerfully and compellingly than ever. I hope the stories herein will demonstrate that, and provide a new and promising map through midlife crisis to all women who seek it.

Part I

◆ ◆ ◆

THE UPHEAVAL
THAT HAS NO NAME

1

✦ ✦ ✦

MIDLIFE CRISIS:

Not Just for Men Anymore

What can we gain by sailing to the Moon
If we are unable to cross the abyss that separates us
from ourselves?

— THOMAS MERTON

Tucked away in a tiny office in the nation's social science nerve center, the University of Michigan's Institute for Social Research, Elaine Wethington is digging for secrets.

Hidden in a mountain of data on the laptop computer before her is the biggest and most systematic study ever of midlife crisis. Professor Wethington, a Cornell University assistant professor on leave for research, is among a team of scholars analyzing the giant MacArthur Foundation "Midlife in the United States" database, an examination of adult development that is unprecedented in its scope and depth. With her own 724-person subset of the study, she expects to lay to rest what scholars increasingly regard as a myth: the notion that midlife crisis is a predictable stage that besets men at a foreseeable time in life, around age 40.

Wethington does indeed lay it to rest—but not in the way she expects. After days of delving into the 770 kilobytes of data, flipping computer pages, merging files, reading printouts, and checking field interviews, she eyes her findings at last—and gasps.

"Omigod. I must have merged the data wrong," she mutters. She runs the numbers again, but the same bombshell emerges:

A startlingly high number of Americans, her study of 724 subjects shows, have experienced what they consider as a midlife crisis, broadly defined as a stressful or turbulent psychological transition that occurs most often in the late forties and early fifties. Twenty-six percent, more than twice the best scholarly estimate of 10 percent, said they had had one.

More surprising is the large percentage of women reporting midlife crises. It has always been assumed by researchers that women develop differently from men. But the data show that by age 50, even more women than men are reporting a turbulent midlife transition: 36.1 percent of women, compared with 34 percent of men.

Applying the findings to the 42 million–member generation of U.S. women who are nearing or in middle age, defined as about 38 to 55 years old, more than 15 million women will have, or are already having, what they regard as a midlife crisis—about equal to the entire populations of Colorado, Massachusetts, and Minnesota combined.

Professor Wethington had discovered the mass upheaval that has no name.

A People's Definition. The same shock of recognition has been expressed by dozens of women who have helped with research for this book. Although the term "midlife crisis" does not always surface immediately, anecdotal tales of middle-aged upheaval abound. Among women's networks, book groups, neighbors, coworkers, relatives, and circles of friends, most women can tell of at least one or two others who have experienced severe midlife turbulence.

The idea of midlife crisis has taken deep root in American culture since it was set forth in scholarly research in the 1960s and 1970s and in Gail Sheehy's popular 1976 book, *Passages*. But most people have not considered it an issue for women. Men around the age of 40, it was believed, stood a strong chance of experiencing a regressive interlude of foolish self-indulgence, sports cars, and younger mistresses, driven by a fear of death. Women were thought to develop differently, their lives shaped by the childbearing and child-rearing cycle, and by menopause. Thus while the male midlife crisis is reflected in literary and film heroes from Shakespeare's Mark Antony to Kevin Spacey's Lester Burnham in *American Beauty*, women have long been relegated to supporting roles as victims or temptresses to their leading men.

Wethington's study was the first scholarly look at midlife crisis in a broad, nationally representative sample, and the definition and scope that emerges is markedly different. Beyond the high incidence of female midlife crisis, the 724 people her researchers interviewed in depth had a new "people's definition" for it. From their perspective, this turbulent transition had little to do with a fear of death. Her subjects saw it in a more flexible and somewhat more positive light, as a challenging situation brought on by major life transitions or events. They also believed that midlife crisis could occur anytime across the entire expanse of middle age right up to retirement, rather than exclusively at or around age 40.[1]

Clearly, mainstream Americans had hijacked the scholarly term from research psychologists and given it their own populist meaning, one that encompasses women and elevates female midlife turbulence into the spotlight. Amid an absence of much public education about adult development, this more flexible definition helps people make sense of the psychic windshear that sends them pitching and rolling in their middle years.

A similar portrait emerges from my own study of the life stories of fifty women who have experienced midlife crisis. The women I interviewed come from nineteen states in the Northeast, South, West, Midwest, and Pacific Northwest, as well as Washington, D.C., and Toronto, Canada. They range from public company executives, attorneys, business owners and managers to real-estate agents, administrative assistants, secretaries, and homemakers. Thirty-nine are mothers. Echoing Wethington's study, their midlife crises began at ages ranging from 39 to 52; the average age was 44.6.

Many events can trigger a midlife crisis, some positive, some negative. Nine women in my study said a liberating event, such as an inheritance, early retirement, or a new religious or spiritual insight or experience, touched off their midlife crises.

It was more common, however, for midlife losses or despair to serve as a trigger. In my study, marital problems, divorce, or extramarital affairs led the list of catalytic events. One woman's midlife crisis began during a birthday party, she says, when she gazed across the room at her drunken spouse of twenty years and wondered, "Who is that person?"

The death of one or more loved ones was the second most common triggering factor. For many, the strain of juggling too many work and family duties for too long fed midlife turmoil. Job problems, the stress of corporate life, or disenchantment over job setbacks or an employer's bad behavior touched off other women's midlife crises. Additional common triggering events: the empty nest or anticipation of it, health problems, and major troubles or disappointment with children.

While these events trigger a variety of feelings, my study shows, they always bear the same underlying message: You are on a path to a place you do not want to go.

Wild Hellion Girls. The months before midlife crises were marked for many by an emotional deadness that set in like smog, blacking out the joy in even the most remarkable moments. Sadness, irritability, or a general unease were other markers. Many women began overreacting to normal stresses and strains. With the darkness came the growing conviction that suppressing deep dreams and desires was no longer worth the sacrifice. Old values and standards of behavior began falling away.

The frustrations that erupt are as diverse as the women themselves. A look, a passing touch, a solitary sexual dream reignite a passion for intimacy. A forgotten yen to see the Himalayas at sunset bursts forth into a full-blown resolve. A thirst to do new, more meaningful work takes center stage, causing a woman to jettison her hard-won career of thirty years. A drive to own and run a company emerges so forcefully in a woman's mind that she mortgages her house and sells most of what she owns to satisfy it.

"I was overcome with the most powerful desire to make sure I did not die unfulfilled," says a California woman looking back on a midlife crisis that began at 50, echoing the feelings of dozens of others I interviewed. Another woman said, "I realized I wasn't in a dress rehearsal. I was in life. If I wanted things to change, it was up to me to change them. Right then."

A period of profound psychological turmoil or unrest may follow. Women told of forsaking careers, racing headlong into bone-crushing accidents, wrecking marriages, or quitting home and hearth. Some plunged into a single-minded pursuit of music, the arts, or photography. Some explored new spiritual paths. Others embraced new adventures such as bungee-jumping or motorcycle-riding. Thirsty for intimacy, or merely for reassurance that they were still attractive, some had love affairs. Others, exerting extreme restraint, kept going through the motions of life as they knew it, but paid a price in the form of depression or hopelessness.

"There's this wild hellion girl in me that wants to come out," says Anna, 54, an administrative manager from a small city who, after leading a settled and respectable life for decades, revived an old dream of becoming a jazz musician by taking up piano lessons and nocturnal club-hopping.* She also had a series of romantic trysts with younger men.

Such stories beg the conclusion that midlife crisis always signals a downward spiral. In most cases, it accomplishes the opposite. Women who undertook creative, constructive pursuits outnumbered those who turned to extramarital affairs, overspending, or despair. In engaging in a searching self-examination and sometimes an overhaul of their lives, these women strived to take control—to make the most of the pluses of middle age, increased personal control and freedom, while limiting the minuses—the risks of declining health, weight gain, and chronic illness. In that, midlife crisis was not so much a fearful effort to fend off the future but a profoundly hopeful reaching inward, into the unconscious, to bring forth parts of themselves. Filtering and refiltering their inner light through the prism of midlife crisis, these women created the rich stories that are told in Part II of this book.

The outcomes of midlife crisis are as diverse as the women in my study. Twenty wound up with new careers, thirteen with new spouses or partners. Eight made extreme sports a fixture of their lives; sixteen did the same with adventure travel. Fourteen plunged with fervor into new hobbies, fifteen into religious pursuits. Some did several of the above. And many made quieter, inner changes, drilling deep into day-to-day experiences to look

---

*All the names of the women in my study have been changed, as have any details that might reveal their identities.

for meaning in each moment. Nearly all say midlife crisis transformed their life outlook, changing, for a time, nearly everything and everyone they touched.

"I feel as if I had two complete and total lives," says Marilyn, looking back on a midlife transition that brought a divorce, a new career as head of her own company and, eventually, a new husband. The second and more fulfilling life, she adds, began at 48 with her midlife crisis.

Why Now? This pattern of female midlife crisis is emerging now because, to put it simply, women are different today. The new roles this giant generation of women carved out for themselves in the last quarter of the twentieth century positioned them perfectly for midlife crises in the twenty-first. For the first time in history, women not only face more of the kind of stresses that tend to bring on midlife crises, but they have the financial muscle, the skills, and the confidence to act out their frustrations and resolve them. In a sense, women are having midlife crises now because they can.

The income of middle-aged women has posted powerful gains in comparison with men's, by many measures. Women's inflation-adjusted full-time earnings have risen 16.8 percent in the past fifteen years, giving them the financial strength needed to act on midlife rebelliousness. Men's comparable earnings have declined 1.7 percent over the same period. Nearly one-third of wives now outearn their husbands, and the proportion of women earning more than $100,000 tripled in the past decade. All this gives women a sense of freedom at midlife. "My successful, satisfying career allowed me to be very independent, with a cocky attitude" that sparked to a full-blown midlife crisis, says a California saleswoman in my study.

Women also have the skills and resources to make career changes or start their dream businesses at midlife if they wish. The proportion of professional jobs held by women, from engineering, law, medicine, and architecture to teaching, writing, and computer science, has grown to 54.7 percent from 51.1 percent in 1990. Women hold nearly half, or 45.9 percent, of all executive, managerial, and administrative jobs, from CEO slots to food-service management, up from 40.1 percent in 1990. Women today are better educated than men, too, earning 58 percent of all college degrees granted, including 59 percent of the master's degrees.[2]

Both of these factors—higher occupational status and education—increase the propensity for a midlife crisis, Wethington's research shows. Both traits foster expectations for a higher quality of life, as well as create a sense of entitlement and a more activist stance in expressing personal frustration.

In another change from the past, an especially stifling brand of stress among today's midlife women provides the spark for this psychological tinderbox. Many working women reach their late thirties and forties exhausted by long hours on the job, a relentlessly demanding workplace, and nonstop juggling of work and family. Like light off a disco ball, these women's energies flicker and fragment across so many demanding roles that they lose focus.

This generation of women feels more harried and oppressed

by daily demands than older women.[3] Working mothers' time to themselves, for self-care or just relaxing, has plunged to a mere 54 minutes a day from 2.1 hours in 1977—less than the 1.3 hours of free time reported by men.[4] In a new study, a Gallup poll shows 57 percent of women 40 through 55 years of age say they lack enough time to do what they want, setting them apart from the 48 percent of the entire random sample of 3,015 Americans who feel that way.[5]

"We have created such a fast-paced, jam-packed life that women are not connecting with themselves and picking up on . . . signs and symptoms" of inner needs, says Diane Sanford, a St. Louis clinical psychologist who teaches at St. Louis University.

Today's midlife women are far more likely than the previous generation to say life has become too complex or out of control. Life is "much too complicated" for 73 percent of today's 40- to 54-year-old women, up sharply from the 55 percent who answered yes to that question fifteen years ago, based on new research by the Yankelovich Monitor. The proportion of women searching for ways to gain more control over their lives has risen, to 69 percent from 60 percent. Reflecting the strain, the percentage who feel a "need to take something to calm my nerves" is up as well, to 29 percent from 23 percent in 1988.[6]

Though satisfying in many ways, the multiple roles many women play in their twenties and thirties can also be so draining that women do not even remember much of what happened. Several in my study described a period of "blackout" during their twenties and thirties. They were so stressed and over-loaded that their lives were a blur.

"Our whole lives were consumed by children and work. I almost can't remember those years," says Sarah, a Tennessee physical therapist who says she embraced a "zombie-like rou-tine" to get through it all. She broke free in a midlife crisis that began at 49 and took up kayaking, rowing, and other sports.

The stresses have become so intense that one expert, Kather-ine Halmi, an author of a Cornell University study on eating disorders and a professor of psychiatry at Cornell's Weill Med-ical College, believes they are a major contributing factor to a burgeoning epidemic of eating disorders among midlife women that has surfaced in the past decade.

In another change from the past, today's women believe they have more at stake as they enter middle age. Midlife females have a full three decades or more of life still ahead of them, on average, compared with the scant few years the average middle-aged woman had left at the turn of the century, when the average life expectancy was forty-seven years. More than three-fifths of women of this generation feel younger than they really are, by seven years on average. This contributes to high expectations of longevity, according to a study by the AARP, Washington, D.C.[7]

Culture Clash. Thus armed and motivated for midlife change, this generation of women might be regarded as an irre-sistible force. Awaiting them as they approach their late thirties and forties, however, is the societal equivalent of an immovable object: a popular culture that treats middle-aged women as if they are beneath notice—beyond beauty, beyond sexuality, beyond leadership.

A curtain of invisibility descends upon these women just as their frustrations and desires begin to soar. "I feel like the invisible person," says Valerie, a 49-year-old corporate manager and mother from Connecticut. "This is a very youth-oriented culture. People look right through us and fail to realize what we have gone through and what we have left to achieve." Paradoxically, she says this just as a midlife crisis, marked by extensive travel and community-service work, is causing her own inner sense of identity to spring forth in rich and vivid relief. "Up to this point, I've been busy being someone's daughter, wife, mother. But at forty-nine, I am now myself," Valerie says.

At work, many women reaching middle age encounter the worst discrimination they have experienced. Beryl, a top-producing New York saleswoman for a large company, says that in her mid-forties even her frequent sales awards cannot prevent her from feeling like an outsider. "When executives think of aggressive salespeople, they think of unattached young men," she says. "Now it's my turn to get the crap kicked out of me."

Her growing sense of alienation at work has triggered a midlife crisis that has her donning a leather jacket and jeans on evenings and weekends and hitting rock concerts and clubs. Immersed in her love of live music and the camaraderie of other fans, Beryl, a married mother of two, feels "like a cool girl again."

The dual blinders of ageism and sexism keep other people

from responding to midlife women as individuals. Carol Landau, a clinical professor of psychiatry at Brown Medical School, Providence, Rhode Island, and coauthor of two books on menopause, tells the story of one of her middle-aged clients, an attractive woman accustomed in her youth to receiving lots of attention. The woman was standing at a deli counter, waiting to order, when the clerk looked right through her and addressed the young girl directly behind her. Feeling diminished, the woman pointed out a little angrily that she had been waiting first, then felt embarrassed that she had to even ask. No wonder "the average woman has trouble aging in our society," Dr. Landau says.

Popular culture reflects more than a little discomfort with any suggestion that midlife women have sex lives. Portrayals tend to be contemptuous. In the 2003 movie *50 First Dates*, the romantic overtures of the middle-aged female assistant in Adam Sandler's veterinary practice play out in humiliating results—a walrus throws up on her, and she is heaved violently into a pool.

Nowhere are the stereotypes more evident than in the cultural crucible of a greeting card shop. Among the birthday cards in one card shop I visited, 15 percent broadcast ageist images or messages. "Act your age!" shrieked one, for women in their forties. "Past my prime!" screamed another. Several cards declare the recipient "Over the Hill," as if life were split by a kind of Continental Divide, dooming any initiatives undertaken after age 40 to certain decline.

Such outdated stereotypes play a major role in stoking women's midlife turbulence.

Shock Waves. Women's midlife crises are already sending tremors through American culture, with ripple effects reaching many sectors, from health care, sports, and travel to women's career choices, education, the arts, religion, and relations between the sexes. Taken together, these patterns form a portrait of a generational tempest.

Midlife women are turning old sex roles upside down. They are dating and having affairs with younger mates—a luxury that used to be regarded as the exclusive province of men. They are having more extramarital affairs and initiating more divorces. And increasingly, they are enjoying vital, active sex lives over the age of 45.

Many women in midlife crisis look for meaning in an intimate love relationship. Some want an emotional closeness of a kind they have never had. Others seek confirmation they are still sexually alluring. "When guys find me attractive, it affirms something in me that I want affirmed," says one 54-year-old woman who, after thirty years of fidelity in marriage, started having serial affairs at midlife with younger men.

Dashing the popular view of midlife as a sexual wasteland for females, many middle-aged women are having abundant sex. A startlingly high proportion of single, middle-aged, college-educated women had two or more sex partners in the prior year—12.1 percent, or one in eight, says Alice Rossi, professor emerita at the University of Massachusetts, based on 1995 data from the 6,432-person MacArthur Foundation's "Midlife in the United States" project, a sweeping study of Americans' health, well-being, and social responsibility at midlife.[8]

That percentage likely has risen since then. Women in their forties today "are going to be much more aggressive in seeking partners" than middle-aged women in the past, says one respected authority, Edward Laumann, sociology professor and lead researcher at the University of Chicago on the 1992 National Health and Social Life Survey, which examined Americans' sexual practices and patterns.[9] Fortified by career clout, financial independence, and the liberated attitudes of a generation that came of age after the 1968–1972 sexual revolution, "women are much more willing to accept the male version of that 'passing fling.'" They are more willing to have sex for pleasure and companionship, says Laumann.

Growing numbers of midlife women are dating younger men, turning old sex roles upside down. Several women in my study dated or had sex with a younger man during their midlife crises. Nationwide, 34 percent of single women ages 40 through 69 dated a younger man in 2003.[10]

A rising number of women are having extramarital affairs. In 1991, research showed married men cheated a lot more often, with about one in five admitting to having affairs, compared with one in ten women. But the latest data from the National Opinion Research Center, from 2002, suggests that the overall rate of extramarital cheating for women is rising rapidly and is approaching that of men, with nearly one in six married women saying they have had affairs.[11]

The middle-aged group appears to be leading that trend. In a look at 1994 data from the National Opinion Research Center, Michael Wiederman found a spike in the rate of cheating reported by women ages 30 to 50, and lower rates among women born before the baby boom.[12] Wiederman, an associate professor of psychology at Columbia College in South Carolina, believes that extramarital sex is simply easier and more acceptable to today's middle-aged women than it was in the past. "There's been a change in attitudes and mores. There are more women out there in the working world, and they have greater independence, which you need to have an affair."

Psychologist Diane Sanford says a growing number of her patients—long-settled women who are part of mainstream culture—are having extramarital affairs as part of "their midlife transition. And these are not the kind of women we would normally expect to be having affairs."

Janet Lever, a leading sex researcher at the University of California at Los Angeles, adds, "Affairs are a luxury item. Midlife women today have the flexibility to have them, and they have money of their own."

Women by some measures are also driving a rise in the divorce rate at midlife. In the past, divorce declined steadily among people in middle age, as partners presumably settled down with advancing age. But the 1990s' divorce rate among women who were in their forties as the decade began rose more than two percentage points to 9.3 percent. That compares with 7.1 percent in the previous decade. Divorce rates for the total population stayed about flat during that time.[13]

In a related shift, two-thirds of women who divorced between the ages of 40 and 70 say they, not their ex-husbands, initiated the breakup. Women in unfulfilling marriages are more willing to chart a new life for themselves; divorce at midlife is no longer the sexual dead-end it used to be for women, says the AARP, which has studied marital breakups at midlife and beyond. Seventy-five percent of divorced women in their fifties reported enjoying a serious relationship after their breakup, often within two years. Among divorced women, researchers see "a sense among most that they were emerging with a new lease on life."[14]

Remarriage rates confirm this; they are steady or increasing among women at middle age.[15] Researchers on marriage at the National Center for Vital Statistics have theorized that women's increasing economic independence over time will make them more likely candidates for remarriage, just as financially successful men have been in the past.

This new self-confidence among midlife divorcées is evident in the workplace. Three-fifths of divorced women in their forties say they enjoy flirting for fun at work, says Janet Lever. More than one-third of divorced women in their forties also admit they play up their sexuality at work, according to Lever's study for *Elle* magazine and MSNBC.com.[16]

Carving New Paths. The midlife search for meaning drives women into other pursuits. Many change careers to pursue work that is more altruistic or fulfilling. Others return to college to pursue a new interest. Part-time college enrollment among women 35 and over grew 10.5 percent in the past decade, nearly twice the overall rate of growth in part-time students.[17] Full-time enrollments among older women rose 31.3 percent, well above the 18.7 percent overall trendline.

Organized religion is drawing significant support from midlife women's quest for meaning. While the proportion of middle-aged men who attend church often has declined nearly ten percentage points in the past decade to 38 percent, women ages 38 through 55 have held steady in church attendance. About half of midlife women continue to attend church at least twelve times a year, according to the DDB Life Style Study, a long-term survey of 4,000 consumers by DDB Worldwide Communications Group, a New York advertising concern.[18] Thirteen women in my study turned at midlife to a deep involvement in religious or spiritual pursuits.

Facing Fears. Midlife women are changing the face of sports and travel, especially in areas not traditionally associated with their age group or sex. Participation in such adventurous pursuits as wilderness camping, wall-climbing, kayaking, and snowshoeing has risen significantly since 1997 among women ages 38 through 55, according to a study conducted for this book by Leisure Trends Group, a Boulder, Colorado, research organization. American Sports Data, of Hartsdale, New York, a provider of sports information, says more midlife women have taken up running in the past fifteen years, while men's participation has fallen.

Middle-aged women are showing more commitment to sports. The proportion of 38- to 55-year-old women who say outdoor or fitness sports are their favorite way to spend time has risen by several percentage points in the past six years to 53 percent. Middle-aged female athletes are ratcheting up the intensity level, too; 41 percent feel strongly about going to any length to finish whatever sporting activity they undertake, up from just 30 percent in 1990.[19]

"These women want to prove to themselves that they can still do it—kayak for four hours, or hike in the mountains for five hours, and challenge their bodies not just physically but mentally as well," says Aidan Boyle, an owner of Body & Soul Adventures, an Ileha Grande, Brazil, operator of retreats emphasizing fitness, adventure sports, and nutrition. No wonder a recent Sony commercial featured a grandmother getting into an underwater cage to take pictures of sharks attacking.

Midlife crisis for Marilyn, a former homemaker and community volunteer, erupted in a drive to conquer her lifelong acrophobia. Swallowing her fear, she climbed to the edge of a cliff, harnessed herself to a steel cable called a zipline, and rode it hundreds of feet from a mountain peak to the ground. "It showed me I could conquer my fear and do anything I wanted," says Marilyn, who went on to found a company.

Another woman in my study, a physical therapist from the South who had always been the last kid chosen for playground games and never participated in sports, took up rowing in an eight-person crew. She overcame both her fears and her sense of inadequacy. The physical challenge "made me evaluate what I was truly looking for," she says.

Middle-aged women are also hopping on that old symbol of

the male midlife crisis—the motorcycle. Thanks in large part to midlife women, female ownership and operation of motorcycles has risen 34 percent in the past five years, far outpacing the overall national growth rate of 23 percent, the Motorcycle Industry Council says.

Midlife women are leading growth in some fitness pursuits too. Free-weight training by women ages 35 through 54 rose sevenfold in the past fifteen years, surpassing participation by midlife men three to one. Females ages 35 to 54 have been joining health clubs at a far faster clip than men. Women in this age group posted a 31 percent gain in memberships in the past 15 years, nearly twice that of men.[20]

The Flip Side. A dark side of all this physical activity among women is an epidemic of eating disorders. When a woman becomes obsessed with fitness at midlife, a compulsion may kick in to "perfect" her body—a cornerstone of eating disorders.

Admissions of women in their forties to the eating disorders program at New York Presbyterian Hospital in Westchester more than doubled in the past decade, to 8.8 percent of all admissions in 1998 from 4.2 percent in 1988.[21]

When the Remuda Ranch treatment facility opened in Wickenburg, Arizona, in 1990, "we saw virtually no cases of eating disorders in middle-age women," says Edward Cumella, research director. But women's midlife turmoil in recent years quickly pushed admissions in that age group to 6 percent of residents in 1998, then to 11 percent in 2004. The need among midlife women is so acute that Renfrew Center, a Philadelphia eating-disorder treatment facility where nearly one-fourth of patients are middle-aged, has started a new residential and day-treatment program for women over 35.

The causes experts cite for eating disorders in mature women echo the causes of midlife crisis: marital discord, the empty nest, career changes, or divorce. Though little research has been done, most explanations center on "cultural changes in the United States that have intensified since 1990," including a general obsession with youth, weight, and bodily perfection, Cumella says.[22]

Eating disorders reflect "an addiction to try to control . . . some feeling, whether it's anxiety, stress, or sadness," says Patricia Saunders, a psychoanalyst with Graham Windham Services to Families and Children in New York City. She is seeing a sharp rise in middle-aged women clients with food-related disorders. "The most common elements I see are the drive for perfection, the mourning of youth or youthful fantasies, the empty nest, and certainly the staggering incidence of divorce."

Once again, women's fear of losing their attractiveness and sex appeal is fueling this dangerous trend. This insecurity surfaces over and over in research on women at midlife as a powerful driver of their sexual satisfaction, use of hormone therapy during menopause, and other behaviors. Fully three-fifths or more of women in their forties and fifties worry about losing their physical appeal, says Professor Alice Rossi of the University of Massachusetts. The proportion has probably risen since that data was collected in 1995.[23]

The insecurities in many women spring from a deeper

unease. Therapists and counselors say they are seeing growing numbers of midlife women as patients. Sanford, the St. Louis psychologist, says one-third to one-half of her large practice is women in tough midlife transitions. Many are wrestling with why they have not yet achieved some of their primary goals in life. "They're asking, 'Who do I want to be now, as I prepare for the next half of my life?'"

These women do not know what they are experiencing when they begin therapy, and they have no name for it, psychologists say. But they are troubled by a vague, pervasive unease. Clients of Marian Frank, a Philadelphia clinical psychologist, "say things like, 'I feel dead inside,' or 'I can't stand my marriage,' or 'I'm working so hard there's no time for anything else,'" Dr. Frank says. "What they really mean—but are not saying—is, 'I don't have any meaning in my life.'"

The frustrations are surfacing in research. Midlife women report more disruptive emotional problems than others. Women 40 through 55 years of age say they experience poor mental or emotional health for 3.9 days a month, 50 percent more than the highest levels among women of other ages, or than men. Their problems interfere more often with day-to-day activities such as work, recreation, or self-care, compared with others, according to research for this book by the Gallup Organization.[24]

An Unprecedented Pattern. All this marks a turning point from the past. Although there is evidence in older research that women of previous generations experienced some turmoil in middle age, nothing emerges on a scale approaching the current trend. A study of late-1950s graduates of Mills College in California demonstrated psychological unrest among the women in their early forties, with most stabilizing by age 52. But for a significant number of these women, the challenge at midlife was finding their way into the labor force—a rare circumstance today.[25]

In another departure from the past, we know for the first time what midlife crisis is not: menopause.

Any turmoil a woman faced at middle age has long been blamed on menopause. Back in the 1950s and 1960s, "The Change" became the scapegoat for nearly any kind of turmoil. No wonder midlife women are in upheaval, the thinking went—not only are they undergoing (or approaching, or recovering from) shifts in their reproductive hormones, but they can no longer have babies. New product lines and vendors sprang up to cater to this market, spawning books, herbal remedies, self-help products, sex aids, and nutritional supplements for menopausal women. This biological phenomenon even had its own touring Broadway play, *Menopause, the Musical*.

There's no question that menopause is difficult for many women. The MacArthur Foundation study found as many as one-third report an increase in hot flashes, sweating, sleeplessness, irritability, and discomfort during sex at some point between the ages of 40 and 55. I have experienced most of these symptoms myself. One of the women in my study, a Dallas financial planner, suffered so much from hot flashes that she sometimes ripped off her shirt and cooked dinner topless.

But new research also shows menopause is not the psychic

and sexual brick wall it has been made out to be. Fewer than 1 percent of women attribute midlife turmoil to menopause, Professor Wethington's research shows. In the MacArthur study, Professor Rossi found menopause is "a benign event" for most women that has been widely misunderstood. A large majority, or 61.6 percent, of postmenopausal women reported feeling "only relief" at having gotten through this transition. Another 23 percent said they had no particular feeling about it at all. Asked if they were concerned about being too old to have more children, fully four out of five women responded, "Not at all." Other researchers have found menopause-related changes account for little of the variance in measures of sexuality among women. And research comparing premenopausal and perimenopausal women on cognitive tasks has found no differences on a variety of tasks, after controlling the results for age.[26]

What *did* top women's list of concerns in the MacArthur study were different issues: the fear of declining health, reported by four in ten women, and, again, the looming fear that they would lose their attractiveness, reported by at least three out of five women.

These findings echo the earlier conclusions of the authoritative Massachusetts Women's Health Study, one of the largest studies of middle-aged women. Most women do not seek professional help with the symptoms of menopause, and they feel overwhelmingly positive or neutral, the study found. The authors warned of the risk that other conditions might go undiagnosed because the symptoms were mistaken for menopause.[27]

Arguably, this is what has happened with female midlife crisis: Women's psychological and spiritual upheavals have been mistaken for menopause symptoms and reduced to a biological phenomenon.

In fact, women's midlife turmoil often reflects a major turning point. It transcends any change in their reproductive systems and defies efforts to explain it away biologically. Just as women's inner lives in the 1950s were more multifaceted than the child-rearing roles they were assigned in that era, women's midlife crises today spring from causes larger than menopause and warrant a more probing look.

Male-Female Differences. As the trend expands, a definition of midlife crisis that encompasses women will become part of the vernacular, and women will put their stamp on the term. Real differences are emerging in how women and men experience midlife crisis, however. A variety of studies suggest that women not only undergo bigger changes than men in middle age, but they also by some measures have a more positive attitude about their prospects in life.

Midlife women are markedly more optimistic than men about retaining their health and vigor into old age; 63 percent of women in their forties and fifties expect to be at least as healthy and active at age 65 as they are now, compared with only 56 percent of men.[28] Midlife women are also more than twice as likely as men to cite "a positive attitude or outlook" as the reason they feel younger than their years.[29]

Women also experience a more dramatic rebound in personal fulfillment at midlife, on the heels of a deeper dip in their child-rearing years. A study by Wethington, Ronald Kessler of the Harvard Medical School, and Joy Pixley of the University of California at Irvine found that only 24 percent of women ages 35 through 49 said they had "fulfilled a special dream" in the past five years, such as acquiring money or property, accomplishing something noteworthy, finding a partner, or getting married. For adult women, this was the lowest ebb of fulfillment in their entire adult lives. By contrast, 40 percent of the men in the same age group reported dream fulfillment.

But the pattern quickly reverses over the age of 50. The study shows 36 percent of women ages 50 through 64 report reaching some fulfilling goal in the preceding five years, suggesting midlife can be a time of powerful renewal for women. In contrast, men's dream fulfillment goes downhill from their mid-thirties on, sinking to 28 percent from ages 50 to 64, and 27 percent after that.[30]

The triggers of midlife crisis reflect sex differences too. Women's midlife crises are more likely than men's to begin with family events or problems, from a divorce or a parent's death to an extramarital affair. Problems related to children are particularly likely to surface as factors, such as realizing you have not met your own standards or goals as a parent.[31]

Whereas male midlife crisis is more likely to be driven by work or career issues. women's turmoil is more likely to be driven by introspection. Women are more likely than men to report major turning points in their lives at midlife.[32] Women are more likely to attribute their midlife crises to some new insight into themselves through religion, therapy, or reflection. Women are more likely to cite personal health problems as the cause of their midlife crises—7.4 percent, compared with just 2 percent for men. This can include worries about slowing down or, again, about losing one's attractiveness.

Perhaps most significant for the culture, women are innately more likely than men to talk with others about their inner turmoil, to openly seek solutions, and to look for remedies in community and society. That suggests their midlife transitions will send increasingly visible ripple effects through society.

Different Demographics. The sheer size of this age group of women ensures the trend will have unprecedented impact. At 41.6 million members, this generation of baby boom women is more than twice the size of the G.I. Joe generation of men who fought in World War II and transformed the U.S. economy, and three times the size of the suffragette generation of women who won the vote in the early 1900s. As midlife crisis unfolds among this giant generation, women will redraw the face of the life-cycle clock, changing expectations about menopause, the empty nest, and women's vitality, sex lives, and creative potential in middle age.

The breadth of the changes they are undergoing will leave few sectors of society untouched. Newly mindful of what anthropologist Margaret Mead called PMZ, or "postmenopausal zest," politicians who once chased soccer moms may start chasing the massive PMV—the postmenopausal vote. Given society's obsession with beauty, women will continue to fuel growth in fitness and dieting products, but they also may spark a cultural rebellion: Just as this generation of women challenged sex roles in the 1960s and 1970s, they may dynamite the age roles deeply rooted in our culture as well. Their spending patterns may well help drive the economy, as the despair and psychological turmoil that often accompany midlife crisis opens women's wallets and dissolves normal inhibitions about spending. Adventure and travel activities tailored to venturesome tastes and physical limitations of women in midlife will grow. These women will also drive expansion in inclusive, humanistic religious and spiritual movements, and in voluntarism.

All the changes will be fueled by this generation's high-octane sense of entitlement. Where their mothers and grandmothers might have kept midlife yearnings to themselves, today's women feel they have a right not only to express their feelings but to act on them. The Yankelovich Monitor's longitudinal study provides evidence of this generational tendency to take charge. The poll shows 67 percent of 40- to 54-year-old women "work hard at coming out on top in every situation, from the least important to the most important," up from 60 percent of middle-aged women in 1988. They also have the backbone needed: Just half say they sometimes see a need to compromise their principles, down from the 56 percent of the previous generation of midlife women who answered yes to that question in 1988, Yankelovich reports.[33]

When midlife yearnings hit, few of these women feel compelled any longer to suppress them. Discouraged by a flagging marriage, missing her adult children, and yearning for fulfillment beyond her job as an administrative manager, Anna, whom we'll meet in the next chapter, woke up one day to the shocking truth that nothing in the life she had built in thirty years of marriage held meaning for her anymore. She would sacrifice anything, she realized, to revive her love for music, and her old dream of making a profession of performing. Echoing the resolve of many women at this life stage, she says, "I'd rather be dead than not live this out."

2

✦ ✦ ✦

THE BREAKING POINT
Why Midlife Crisis Has So Much Power

Rivers in extremely cold climates freeze over in winter.
In the spring, when they thaw, the sound of ice
cracking is an incredibly violent sound. The more
extensive and severe the freeze, the more thunderous
the thaw. Yet, at the end of the cracking, breaking,
violent period, the river is open, life-giving, life-
carrying. No one says, "Let's not suffer the thaw; let's
keep the freeze; everything is quiet now."

—MARY E. MEBANE,
Mary, Wayfarer: An Autobiography

No one who knows Anna by day would expect to find her lying by night on a blanket on the grass with a young lover. Alone with a man twenty years younger, relaxing by a lake under a starlit summer sky, Anna herself is disbelieving.

At age 54, she never expected to hear again what she is hearing from the virile, muscular man across from her—that she is sexually attractive. She did not expect to feel what she is feeling—romantic, excited, eager.

A pillar of respectability in her small city, Anna has worked hard for decades at her job and her marriage. By all appearances, she is steadfast and reliable. She has been faithful to her husband for more than twenty years, loving to her children, and diligent in her job as an administrative manager.

But this night, another side of Anna is in charge. It is the side of her that has begun frequenting jazz clubs alone at night over the objections of her husband, that craves sexual excitement and affirmation, that yearns to be a jazz performer and producer. After a chance encounter at a club with the young man, a friend from work, she has begun taking evening walks with him. Now, the attraction she feels for him is too strong to resist.

Shielded by darkness, they have sex. Afterward, her young lover holds Anna, caressing her. "I cannot believe we did that," she murmurs. Her mind will replay the encounter for weeks.

It's Now or Never. The tryst is one symptom of a stormy midlife crisis that has Anna careening from euphoria to black despair. Somewhere along the way, while she was chalking up three decades of respectable living as a wife, mother, and manager, she lost her connection with herself.

Now, at midlife, frustration over her stagnant marriage, dead-end career, and empty nest have sparked an eruption of feelings Anna thought she had left behind years ago. She is tired of smiling at customers at work when she does not feel like it, tired of working all day and coming home to a second shift, tired of her husband's sitting on the couch and clicking the remote when she yearns for more. She is overwhelmed by desires to enjoy and make the music she loves, to experience deeper intimacy, and to forge relationships with people who share her passions.

Anna has hit the breaking point—a juncture when keeping up old values, goals, and dreams no longer seems worth the effort. At this critical time, the impulses, desires, losses, and strains of midlife mount to such proportions that a woman begins, consciously or unconsciously, to depart from her old path and to leave parts of her life behind. She may experience the breaking point as liberating and energizing, or as a descent into despair. Either way, she will never be the same.

Anna knows her behavior is jeopardizing her marriage; a part of her does not want to destroy it. "I don't want to throw away everything that's dear to me," Anna says. "But this driven nature just takes over." She will skid to the brink of suicide before she is done.

Anna's story is an extreme, somewhat melodramatic example of the powerful turbulence and risk taking that can erupt in midlife crisis. These forces can jeopardize a lifetime of work building a reputation, a marriage, a career.

While most women experience more measured, gradual changes than Anna, midlife crisis in all cases draws its power from roots reaching deep into our sense of who we are. A feeling of urgency arises: Now is the time to either fulfill your dreams, or give them up. To respond is to cast a lifeline to drowning parts of ourselves.

The energies that drive midlife crisis spring from hopes, wishes, and goals that have been repressed. When these parts of ourselves reemerge, they take on great power. That we have shoved them underground for a time—to win that corner office, to raise our kids, to pay the bills, to draw about us the mantle of adult responsibility and respectability—does not diminish their potency. "Life still clings strongly to them. And actually the seeds of the future lie in these neglected" aspects of oneself, writes psychoanalyst Murray Stein.[1]

A Model Child. Anna had plenty of inhibitions to cast aside. The oldest of four children, she strived in childhood to be perfect. Her parents cared a lot about their image in the community. Raised by the rule "We do everything right," Anna heeded her parents' warnings that others would be quick to judge the whole family by her behavior.

By all appearances, her family seemed content. Her mother and father kept up a facade of happy marriage. But her father transferred often for his job. Uprooted again and again, Anna had a lonely childhood. "I had to make new friends all the time," she says. She learned to be friendly under any circumstances: "I could make conversation with a doorknob."

Nevertheless, with all the moves, she spent a lot of time alone in her room listening to the radio. "I would sing and sing and sing, and I absolutely loved it. That was my salvation. I imagined myself in those songs and I imagined people singing those songs to me," she says. Music was a river connecting her to an imagined intimacy with others, and to the freedom to express herself.

Anna dropped out of college to marry young, to a successful and popular man in her community who was ten years older. Her husband was handsome and well-known—a fine catch, stoking the family pride in appearances.

She buried the music-loving part of herself and plunged into adulthood, earning a living, tending her marriage, raising the children they soon had. Her husband had a rewarding career that required education and skill, but fell short of paying enough to support the family well. Lacking a college degree, Anna found herself working full-time in jobs she found dull. She felt trapped doing the same tasks over and over.

Both she and her husband were committed to making their marriage work, and they got counseling when they had trouble with communication and sex. Nevertheless, over the years, Anna resented the stresses of cooking, cleaning, and doing laundry on top of her daytime job. Her husband had it "so damn easy," she would think.

Her husband did a few household chores and was a devoted father. But in Anna's eyes, he mostly failed at intimacy. At critical moments, when she was sick or exhausted and asked for help, he brushed her aside. He routinely gave his work top priority. She yearned for encouragement she never got from him, reassurances that she was attractive and sexually alluring.

Beginning in her forties, Anna receives a series of blows. Her beloved father dies, and her three children leave home and settle down on their own, unmarried, leaving a void. Again, as in childhood, Anna feels uprooted. Her husband's job has taken her far from her extended family. Watching friend after friend enjoy the birth of grandchildren, she battles a mounting despair.

Driving across a bridge one day near her city, her eyes leap to a guardrail she had passed hundreds of times—a flimsy barrier between the road and the abyss. Dozens of feet below churn the turbulent waters of a river. The thought of ending her pain flickers to mind, then sparks into a flash fire.

"It would be so easy to just veer off. I don't think anybody would really miss me," she thinks, tears coursing down her cheeks. She pulls her car over and sobs, wishing she had the will to hurtle through the guardrail. Struggling for control, she tells herself her children would mourn her. But her husband would doubtless remarry quickly.

Anna is stunned at how indifferent she is to the idea.

Breaking Free. Shaken by her brush with suicide, Anna begins feeling a new rebelliousness. "I don't want to be stuck in this box I've been in. I don't want to be always wondering what people are thinking about me. I want to let the chains fall off."

She signs up for weekly piano lessons with a young musician. In the artificial intimacy of his tiny studio, Anna picks up the first signals that she is still sexually alluring—from her teacher, a man fifteen years her junior. His interest is like a drug. For the first time in decades, she feels attractive, and they have a brief affair.

"For years I've gone the extra mile and turned the other cheek and believed there was really a reason for it. I've not worn my feelings on my sleeve," she says. "Now, damn it, I just want to wear my feelings on my sleeve. . . . I'm tired of being the person who follows all the rules."

The teacher provides an entrée to a new circle of friends, musicians, and music lovers. Anna starts frequenting clubs, staying after midnight, losing herself in the music. The jam sessions so energize her that when she returns home, she stays awake hours longer, to make music of her own on the piano.

Her vitality draws other admirers. She has a new affair, with the young man from work. Anna takes a new teacher, an accomplished musician, and thrills to his encouragement. When he sings along with her playing, she feels as close to heaven as life can bring her. "The part of me that comes alive is really about the music," she says.

Anna dreams of a career in music, as a promoter for jazz groups. She talks about the idea with a prospective business partner, an experienced publicist, who is pressuring her to form a partnership. But Anna does not even tell her husband about her dream. She believes he would only discourage her, saying, "What makes you think you can do that?" Still, watching jazz artists perform, Anna aches to pour out her heart as fully. "There are so many things I want to do. There's not enough time," she says.

Into the Void. Women in midlife crisis at first enter a kind of void. Facing a stagnant marriage, the death of her father, and an empty nest, Anna no longer sees any point in repressing her love of music or her desire for intimacy. But the crumbling of her old facade—the persona—allows chaos to erupt.

This marks a threshhold of development—a transitional or liminal stage. Washington, D.C., psychiatrist Lise Van Susteren likens the experience to setting out to sea in a boat after being moored for a time: "The ship has been safe in the harbor. But that's not what ships are made for. In order to stay alive, to stay excited about life, we need to move out into choppy waters."

Liminality is often marked by extremes of emotion and behavior. When half of your off-hours pursuits require a full-face helmet, as happened in my midlife crisis, for example, or when you have trouble sitting still at your desk without being overwhelmed by sexual fantasies, you have entered liminality.

Its power is illustrated by the age-old Baltic folktale recounted in Clarissa Pinkola Estes's 1992 bestseller, *Women Who Run with the Wolves*. In a story that has been told and retold for generations, Estes writes of a little girl's encounter with the enchantress-hag Baba Yaga. The dilemma in this tale is that the home fires have gone out. The coals on the hearth where the child, Vasalisa, lives unhappily with her cruel and hateful stepmother have been allowed to grow cold. Hoping that Vasalisa will be killed, the stepmother sends her on a dangerous journey to the fearsome hovel of Baba Yaga, deep in the dark forest, to retrieve coals to rekindle the fire.

Baba Yaga, who represents a kind of wild psychic teacher, agrees to give Vasalisa the coals—but only if she completes a series of seemingly impossible tasks, laundering, cleaning, clearing, sorting food, and cooking. The penalty for failing, Baba Yaga says, is to be eaten by the hag. As Vasalisa lives with Baba Yaga for a time, the child learns to face the great power of the wild goddess. With the help of a wise doll Vasalisa carries in her pocket, a gift from her dead mother, the child manages to mediate Baba Yaga's demands. She accomplishes them without being consumed by them.

Although the hag seems cruel and frightening, she is fair:

When Vasalisa finishes the heroic tasks she is assigned, Baba Yaga gives the child a fiery human skull to reignite her home fires and sends her on her way. Guided by light from the skull, Vasalisa finds a path through the dark forest, arrives home, burns her hateful stepmother to ashes, and lives long and well thereafter.

Vasalisa's ordeal represents the hardships we all face in caring for our inner selves, Estes writes. Baba Yaga is teaching the child how to maintain the psychic house of the feminine. To stoke our inner powers, we must cleanse our emotions, sort and renew our values, tidy up our thinking, and nourish and build energies within ourselves. In compelling Vasalisa to face the fearsome power of the feminine and accomplish these tasks without perishing, Baba Yaga is training her to rekindle the passions and powers of her own soul.

"A woman must be willing to burn hot, burn with passion, burn with words, with ideas, with desire for whatever it is that she truly loves," Estes writes. "It is the cooking up of new and completely original things, of new directions, of commitments to one's art and work, that continuously nourishes the wild soul." The penalty for allowing those inner fires to grow cold is to endure the deathly rage of the Yaga, the wild mother and teacher. "There's hell to pay if she goes hungry," Estes says.[2]

Reclaiming the Fire. Similarly, there's hell to pay if a woman's need for purpose and meaning lies dormant too long. The process of stoking these inner fires, called "serving the non-rational" by

Estes, is a defining task of midlife crisis. To continue to grow as a human being, a woman has no choice but to make whatever journey is necessary to rekindle her inner passions.

Anna's midlife odyssey brings her a good deal of inner pain, shame, and guilt. Her husband is dismayed by her passion for late-night jazz. But he refuses to accompany her to the clubs, and she craves the music and the companionship of others who share her interest. Anna's extramarital affairs are brief and emotionally wrenching. Her husband does not know about them, but Anna agonizes over being disloyal and potentially hurting him. Her conscious goal is not to tear apart her marriage. She does not want to be alone in old age. But that mindfulness is drowned out by the urgency she feels.

She likens her mind-set to that of an out-of-control teenager. "I am experiencing things I should have experienced back then. Now, I am playing catch-up," she says.

Many people in midlife crisis wonder how they can feel so bad at such a mature stage of life. The answer, says Elaine Wethington, the Cornell University researcher: "Growth hurts."

A Puzzle for Loved Ones. Midlife crisis can open a Los Angeles-sized chasm between who you think you are, and who others see you to be. Giving birth to lost parts of ourselves compels us to set aside, for a time, the roles, image, goals, habits, and behaviors that have made up the persona—the social facade that seems to others to make up the entire personality, but that may really be only part of it.

People in midlife crisis sometimes behave in shocking ways

that seem out of character. They do not realize how they appear to others. Driven by intense emotion, moodiness, or impulsiveness, we believe we look more romantic, dashing, youthful, powerful, or wise than we really are. We may also believe that newfound lovers, teachers, or other "midlife messiahs" are more romantic, dashing, youthful, powerful, or wise than they really are. We see what we want to see.

Anna has not told even her closest friends about all of her escapades; she knows they would be shocked. Her husband finds her behavior baffling. He tolerates her nocturnal outings only because he cannot dissuade her.

"I'm going to give in. I don't have to like it, but I'm not going to say anything about this anymore," he says. He is no longer attracted to Anna, he tells her, and they have begun sleeping in separate rooms. "I liked you better when you were how you used to be," he says.

"I can't be that anymore," she replies.

Anna is worried by the rift. "It's terribly sad to me [that midlife yearnings] are not what's good for my relationship with my husband. It's like I'm throwing everything out the window." But her focus at the moment is within. "Emotionally, I have packed my suitcase in my thoughts, over and over," she says.

Subject of Satire. This kind of turmoil can be so unsettling to others that they use humor as a defense, making fun of midlife crisis in order to remove themselves to a safe psychological distance. People hide behind self-righteousness or derision largely because it is scary to think that they, too, could be harboring reckless inner needs that may take the driver's seat at any time. The socially disruptive, seemingly irrational behavior is alarming because it could happen to you.[3] This is a prospect many people would rather hold at bay—with humor, condemnation, skepticism, or whatever defense does the trick.

As the phenomenon of female midlife crisis grows, expect plenty of cultural satire on the subject. Fashion writer Dany Levy coined a new term to describe a woman who is "way too old for what she is wearing, as in, 'That 45-year-old woman is wearing low-cut jeans. Is she crazy or just teenile?'"[4]

Already, motorcycle-riding grannies populate the shelves of greeting card shops. In Jared Hess's brilliant 2004 film satire about teen life, *Napoleon Dynamite*, the hero's grandmother, a woman who is probably in her fifties, dons a T-shirt reading "DIVORCED" and takes to the beach in a dune buggy. Flying over a hilltop to the applause of a gaggle of ripped, bronzed beachboys, Grandma crashes at breakneck speed and cracks her coccyx.

In my most turbulent stage, my daughter, then fifteen, kidded me about leaving her no behavioral limits to rebel against. "How am I going to have my own teenage rebellion when you're already acting crazy?" she said jokingly. "I can see it all now: I'll call home from college and say, 'Mom, I'm dating the Unabomber.' And you'll say," she adds, affecting a falsetto voice, "'That's lovely, Dear. Did you smoke some weed?'"

We do not do drugs and my daughter, fortunately, is not dating a Unabomber type. But her teasing reflects frustration over her playing the adult role at times during my midlife crisis, begging me not to go bungee-jumping or take foolish risks on our ATVs.

Finding the Middle Way. Like Vasalisa, who managed, with the help of the wise doll from her mother, to reclaim her inner fire without dying at the hands of the sorceress, the challenge in midlife crisis is to integrate lost parts of ourselves without destroying the pieces of our old lives that are worth keeping. The goal should be a delicate balance between restraint and exploration. We must take our needs seriously, without losing a healthy suspiciousness of the siren song of the new people and pursuits that beckon.[5]

Abiding this tension between growth and safety is not an easy path. Some psychological theories offer perspective. (For more on the checkered history of midlife crisis in the annals of psychological theory, please see Appendix A.) Pioneering psychologist Erik Erikson is famous for his theory, set forth in the 1950s, that people develop not only in childhood and adolescence, as Freud believed, but throughout adult life. Each of the eight stages of development Erikson described brings new tasks for a person to master. And in each stage, people experience tension between opposing traits—developing trust versus mistrust in infancy, for example. While we need to be trusting, we also need a little bit of mistrust to keep us from being naive or gullible. Thus a healthy person learns to strike a balance.

The stages of early and middle adulthood present two sets of developmental tasks, Erikson said. The first, in young adulthood, is to find equilibrium between intimacy—your ability to be close to others as a lover, a friend, and a member of society—and isolation. While we need intimacy, we also need to sustain enough separation to avoid becoming promiscuous or losing ourselves in others.

In middle adulthood, the time between one's mid-twenties and late fifties, Erikson believed, the task is to develop generativity. This means the ability to contribute to the welfare of future generations, without necessarily expecting a return on that investment. In the opposite task, adults must resist the tendency to stagnate and become self-absorbed, caring for no one but themselves. Thus a healthy midlife adult will learn to give freely to society and to future generations, while balancing that giving with attention to her own needs and self-care.

Anna, for example, seems to be wrestling with both of Erikson's developmental tasks of early and middle adulthood. She is looking for intimacy in her extramarital romances. But she is also trying to strike a balance, to keep from losing herself in promiscuity. "It is really hard to control this beast," she says, "but I am learning."

Anna is also moving toward generativity. If she were to realize her dream career as a producer and promoter, she could help young musicians express their creativity—a fulfillment denied her in her own youth. But in this, too, she needs to strike a balance by safeguarding her ability to make a living—the viewpoint she sees her husband articulating, too harshly, when she imagines him raining down contempt upon her dreams.

Another psychological viewpoint is found in Jungian psychology. This theory says that buried or repressed parts of our personalities, called "the shadow," may emerge at midlife. In men, this is the "anima," or the repressed feminine side. In women, it is the "animus," the repressed male side—the "inner teenage boy" that some women in my study tell of experiencing for the first time during midlife crisis. Jungian psychologists draw on mythology and dreams to help interpret repressed parts of the self.

A parable explaining the dynamics of midlife turmoil, from a Jungian standpoint, can be found in Murray Stein's brilliant interpretation of Homer's *Odyssey*.[6] Odysseus's encounter with the enchantress Circe is a lesson in how to form the right relationship with repressed parts of ourselves. While Odysseus is a man striving to integrate his unconscious feminine side, or anima, the same principles hold true for women integrating repressed parts of themselves.

By this interpretation, Odysseus's trek home to Ithaca after a decade spent fighting the Trojan War symbolizes a journey toward psychological wholeness—called *individuation* in Jungian psychology. On Circe's island, however, Odysseus's men hit an obstacle. They are distracted by the siren song of the wild love goddess, Circe, and she entices, enchants, and drugs them, then turns them into pigs—beasts that still have the minds of men, trapped in pig's bodies. In the myth, Circe represents the anima, the repressed female part of the male personality—so powerful as to threaten enslavement. The pigs symbolize humans at their worst, slaves to their lowest impulses. They represent any person trapped in the greedy self-gratification of an out-of-control midlife crisis.

Odysseus wants to avoid the same fate. But he does not want to abandon his men. How can he find a middle path—freeing his men, without falling prey to the wiles of Circe? In Jungian terms, he needs to work out a new kind of relationship with the unconscious part of himself.

Odysseus meets Hermes, a wise guide, who offers a medicine that protects him from Circe's potions, and advice on how to overcome the goddess. Rather than succumbing to her, Odysseus draws his sword and rushes Circe, frightening her into inviting him to bed with her. Only after Odysseus has gained control of the relationship do they make love. Circe then does as Odysseus wants, lifting the spell on his men and freeing them from their bestial trap. The travelers rest on the island for a year, regaining their strength in peaceful relationship with Circe, before continuing their journey.

Just as Odysseus finds a new way to relate to the repressed feminine side of himself, women in midlife crisis have to find a new relationship to their own resurgent traits, needs, and desires. These needs are guideposts to future happiness. But women must not plunge mindlessly into impulsive self-gratification either, losing themselves in casual sex, wild spending, reckless adventures, or destructive treatment of others. Therein lies the core challenge of midlife crisis: to find the middle way.

In Anna's case, rejecting the parts of her personality that are emerging, the lover and the artist, would force her to revert to her old persona. While that would be far safer than the path she has chosen, it also would mean aborting her midlife growth and descending into another kind of hell—a lifetime spent recycling the same old dead-end experiences, the pattern that carried her to the bridge, to the brink of suicide. "The single biggest mistake people make is in not having that midlife crisis. It is a signal that you want more out of life. What a great thing!" says Dr. Van Susteren.

"But," the psychiatrist adds, "that energy has to be used wisely." To give full rein to her shadow side would drive Anna to a different kind of slavery to her physical cravings and passions. Somehow Anna must find a way to approach these needs as Odysseus did—with her sword raised, taking control before welcoming them into her life and her heart. Just as Vasalisa's wise doll helped her find a safe way to reclaim her inner fire, a guide like Hermes—a good therapist, a trusted friend or family member, a spouse or a spiritual advisor—can help us find the middle path: learning from Circe without destroying ourselves.

Frontiers of the Brain. Most of the research so far on these dynamic transitions in adult development at midlife has been done by psychologists. However, new discoveries in cognitive neuroscience support the behavioral evidence that growth and development can reignite in middle age.

In the past, the brain was thought to be fully formed and incapable of further growth after the first few years of life. However, in what amounts to a revolution in neuroscience, researchers are finding that the normal, healthy brain can change and grow new synapses—contact points between cells—throughout the entire life span, says Gene D. Cohen, director of the Center on Aging, Health, and Humanities at George Washington University. Based on studies on animals and human cadavers, the number of synapses can increase by as much as 20 percent in response to new challenges and endeavors undertaken by an adult. Brain cells can also increase in size and sprout additional dendrites, the extensions that make connections with other cells. In response to new challenges, a person's environment and experience at midlife, then, can actually bring about physiological changes in the brain, says Cohen, who is writing a book on the significance of these discoveries for our understanding of how adults develop. The brain responds to mental exercise in much the same way that a muscle responds to physical exercise.[7]

Most research so far has focused on brain development in children and the aged. However, as new research unfolds at the National Institutes of Health and other centers of neurological exploration, more evidence is likely to emerge that the behavioral changes and psychic growth we undergo at midlife are reflected in actual, measurable changes in our brains.[8] Thus in theory, at least, midlife crisis can actually serve to produce a more seasoned, fully developed brain.

Hardwired for Crisis. Why do some women have turbulent midlife crises like Anna's, while others sail through middle age on placid seas? No one has a perfect childhood. Everyone experiences some losses in adult life. And most people have at least some growing pains in middle age. But certain life circumstances and traits increase the odds that you will be among the 36 percent of women who eventually will have what they regard as midlife crises.

People with unsatisfying or all-consuming careers or stagnant marriages are prime candidates. Women whose work/family juggling acts have crowded out all other pursuits from their lives are ripe for turmoil too. People who avoid the need for renewal in work or personal life, who bear down just to "keep on keeping on" and ignore pent-up frustrations, have a higher likelihood of midlife crisis.

People who are carrying a lot of emotional baggage from childhood are also at higher risk. Anna was carrying a truckload of freight in this regard. Not only was her childhood confining, but her parents' marriage served as a model of frustration. Although her mother and father kept up an appearance of marital contentment, Anna later learned they seldom had sex and her father, a passionate man, had to repress himself within the marriage. "He could have been a fun, wild and crazy person, but he was never allowed to be," Anna says. Like her father, she wound up suppressing deep passions that found no outlet in married life. She suspects he, too, had extramarital affairs.

People who exhibit what psychologists call "neuroticism," or a tendency toward instability in their emotions, interactions, and relationships, are more likely to have a midlife crisis. These people tend to become more upset over daily stressors and interactions. Other research has found that depression, a malady which occurs nearly twice as often in women as in men,[9] is linked to a higher likelihood of midlife turbulence.

Other traits increase the odds that you will have a successful midlife crisis—that you will emerge happier, having integrated the changes you desire into your life. Women who tend to dwell on positive events in their lives, rather than negative ones, have a significantly higher chance of making the life changes that will enable them to emerge from midlife more satisfied and success-ful, according to a 1999 study.[10] Not surprisingly, researchers have found those with a high degree of "personal efficacy," or life competencies such as communication, relationship, and work skills, have a higher chance of making positive changes.

Juggling a lot of roles in young adulthood is also linked to successful midlife growth. Two separate studies of a previous generation of women college graduates, one at the University of Michigan and one at Radcliffe College, found the number of roles a woman is playing at age 28 predicts her life satisfaction and well-being at midlife. That is, a woman who is juggling many work, family, and community roles in her late twenties is far more likely in her forties and fifties to find satisfaction, even if she has reduced her obligations by then. This giant generation of women—the most practiced role jugglers yet—may then stand a higher chance than any before it of emerging from midlife crisis fulfilled.[11]

The same two long-term studies suggest the decisions women make as they enter middle age determine their happiness years later. A large percentage of women in the studies—34 percent at Radcliffe and 61 percent at Michigan—expressed regrets of some kind at age 37 about their life course so far. Some chose to use those regrets as fuel to redirect their lives and make changes. By their mid-forties, these women reported at a new round of inter-views that they were just as happy as those who had had no regrets at all when they were 37.

Others among the women who had regrets at 37, however, chose to do nothing about it. These women were unhappiest of all at the next round of interviews. They suffered lower well-being, more depression, and a feeling of being less effective in life, researchers found.[12]

Thus turbulence in middle age is like a flashing neon sign warning travelers to find a new route on life's highway. Beyond lies a fork in the road.

This crossroads presents choices that are fundamental indeed. What is the meaning of life? What is my truest and highest potential? How am I to live out my final years? Striving to answer these questions brought many of the women in my study a time of deep psychological healing. This process is regarded by Jungian psychologists as so profound that it is essentially a spiritual or religious quest. On many levels, that has been my experience.

At the root of the human experience at midlife, the fundamental choice is clear. We can consciously embrace change and move forward. We are hardwired to strive for wholeness.

Or we can deny and repress midlife turmoil—and be driven forward eventually anyway, as the stories in this book will show, by our unconscious pain.

The decision is ours.

Part II

✦ ✦ ✦

THE ARCHETYPES:
LOOKING FOR
OUR MISSING PIECE

In Shel Silverstein's classic children's fable, "The Missing Piece," the hero, a rolling circle missing a sizable chunk, wanders tirelessly in search of its lost wedge.

"Oh, I'm lookin' for my missin' piece!" it sings. In the search, the hero learns that much of life's meaning lies not in attaining a particular goal, but in savoring the journey.

Like Silverstein's wandering hero, women in midlife crisis are searching for a missing part of themselves—a powerful, repressed capability or character trait they are yearning to unearth, express, and integrate into a richer life.

All women are not looking for the same missing piece. Some are seeking love, leadership, or a spiritual mission or meaning, while others want nothing more than artistic self-expression or adventure. Many want a combination of these experiences.

In my study, the driving force behind midlife crisis fell into six broad categories, or archetypes. Each of these desires are to some extent universal, reflecting our core human capabilities to love, to create, to lead, to nurture, and to learn. A particular archetype tends to emerge in a woman's midlife crisis if it is both strong within her, and long repressed. Her experience may rest upon more than one archetype, or upon several in succession.

Each woman's midlife crisis also unfolded at its own rate of speed and with varying degrees of explosiveness and intensity. I have organized these patterns into six basic modes. Understanding the modes of midlife crisis will help women relate to others in transition.

The Archetypes of Midlife Crisis

The Adventurer. Many women seek the catharsis of physical adventure or bold travel at midlife. In endeavors ranging from skydiving to hiking in the Andes, the woman in the Adventurer role strives to conquer her fears and transcend old limits. She plunges into extreme physical effort or into the detachment and freedom of travel, escaping anxieties and compulsions and probing her own personal limits. The Adventurer enlarges her world, encourages risk taking, and vanquishes fear.

The Lover. Many women seek a soul mate at midlife—a lover who promises a chance of attaining complete psychological intimacy. This archetype bears the hope, the seeking, and the building of a life partnership to fulfill that desire. It motivates some women to work on their existing marriages, to draw closer to their partners. Others find a new partner who seems to promise unprecedented intimacy. Women drawn to the Lover role sometimes enter a series of relationships at midlife, each one healthier and more fulfilling than the last. The Lover also sparks formation of more intimate friendships at midlife, affording women the freedom to be spontaneously, unabashedly themselves.

The Leader. Many women seek to make their mark on the world at midlife. They want to get past others' rules and their own people-pleasing behavior to create something new and uniquely their own. The Leader longs to influence others. These are the women who start businesses or political or charity movements at midlife. Some quit repressive jobs to escape leaders they no longer respect. The Leader seizes the opportunity to leave a meaningful legacy.

The Artist. The Artist organizes her life around self-expression, usually in art. She sets aside other pursuits to give number-one priority to her drama, music, writing, sculpture, painting, filmmaking, or acting. To support herself, she may become a teacher of art or take a second job. But there is no question that making her art, and living out her life as an artist, occupy center stage. Her primary joy arises from growing in creativity, manifesting her vision, and uplifting or stimulating others with her work.

The Gardener. Like the hero in Voltaire's classic eighteenth-century novel, *Candide*, the Gardener has traveled the world, discovered much evil, and come to a time of discouragement and disillusionment. At midlife, she concludes that the best path to wisdom lies in tending her own garden, a metaphor for the immediate world within her control. The Gardener focuses deeply on the elements of the life she already has and moves to expand and strengthen them. She strives to make the most of home, family, friends, community, and existing pursuits. She looks within herself to find meaning and new realms of discovery. Above all, this archetype helps a woman learn to cherish and live deeply in the moment.

The Seeker. This archetype motivates a woman to begin her midlife search where other women end theirs: searching for a spiritual path. Regardless of her religious affiliation or background, the Seeker ascribes central importance to finding a set of spiritual beliefs and practices that afford her meaning and serenity. She may spend a great deal of time trying out various religious traditions and teachings before settling on a particular set of beliefs. Some women get deeply involved in an established church. Others hew to nontraditional spiritual disciplines, attending seminars or practicing meditation. Regardless of a woman's individual path, the Seeker has the potential to foster a profound and sweeping life transformation—in attitudes, in career, in love, in hobbies, on all fronts.

The Modes of Midlife Crisis

Each woman's midlife crisis unfolds along a distinct trajectory, at varying speeds, and with unique ups and downs. If archetypes are the direction-setting compass for midlife crises, then modes are the laws of physics governing how they unfold. The women in my study experienced six major modes of transition:

Sonic Boom. This kind of midlife crisis erupts with seismic force and speedily tears apart old relationships, habits, and commitments. Like the aviation phenomenon that lends it its name, a Sonic Boom shakes a woman's world as she breaks through old barriers, then propels her to a new, more energetic plane. The Sonic Boom crisis is the type most often noticed—and satirized—in our culture because it produces behavior out of character with a woman's previous facade, or persona.

Moderate. A woman in this mode transforms her life in a slower, more restrained way. A Moderate crisis entails less conflict and destruction than other models. It allows integration of repressed passions into a woman's personality piece by piece, step by step, without dynamiting her life. This mode eliminates the need for a blowup and may be the healthiest model of all.

Slow Burn. Reluctant to act upon her deepest passions, a woman in this mode "trades down" to more socially acceptable outlets. She resists radical cures, such as embarking on a new career or climbing the Himalayas. Instead, she funnels her energies into smaller or more timid changes. The difference between a Moderate crisis and a Slow Burn is that in the latter, a woman does not honestly address her needs. Instead, she at least partly represses them out of fear. The Slow Burn avoids startling others or doing violence to existing relationships. But it also risks choking off a woman's full potential.

Flameout. In a pattern that can be tragic, a woman in Flameout mode seizes a new life or love only to lose courage midstream and attempt a retreat. Often it is too late; the damage is done, and she has lost a marriage or other valued aspects of life worth keeping. Fear is a driving emotion in a Flameout crisis, causing a woman to make panicky or foolish moves she lacks the skills or self-knowledge to carry out. Her midlife crisis is essentially stillborn, leaving her stuck far short of her potential.

Meltdown. This mode is marked by out-of-control emotion. It generates so much heat and passion that, as in a Flameout, a woman rockets into a new marriage, career, or other endeavor too fast. She may be too eager to ease her pain or too slow to look inside herself for the roots of her problems. Later, she realizes she has repeated the mistakes of the past, unconsciously picking a new partner, career, or other pursuit that is just like the one(s) she threw overboard. Unlike a Flameout crisis, however, a woman in Meltdown eventually makes significant progress toward overhauling her life, albeit on a halting and emotionally messy path.

The Non-Starter. Like Shakespeare's tragic hero Hamlet, the Non-Starter is afraid to act. She becomes mired in indecision about whether "to be or not to be"—to heed her inner voices and "suffer the slings and arrows of outrageous fortune," or to die a psychic death by renouncing them. The Non-Starter does not bring her midlife crisis to fruition at all, but remains trapped in the inaugural stages of despair and discouragement. Her hesitancy dooms her to stagnation; her inability to act becomes an obstacle to decisiveness and growth. Thus midlife opportunities pass her by.

The six chapters that follow will show how these archetypes and modes play out in women's lives.

3

✦ ✦ ✦

THE ADVENTURER

Never let what you fear intrude on what you know.

— Native American saying

The wooden sidewalk ends in a void, jutting off a bridge 141 feet above the aquamarine waters of New Zealand's Kawarau River.

This gangplank to nowhere is actually the launching platform for one of the world's biggest bungee jumps. But to Lynn, age fifty-two, it looks like a gallows.

"Let go of the rail and walk out to the edge," the bungee master says.

"WHAT?" Lynn shrieks to herself. Shoulder-length blond hair lifting in the wind, legs lashed together in bungee harness, Lynn feels nausea roil her stomach. Taking meek baby steps to the edge, she feels like Marie Antoinette being marched to the guillotine.

A voice inside her head—what Lynn calls her "inner teenage boy"—issues a command: "It's now or never, baby." Another voice, Lynn's "staid, sedate house matron," is demanding attention; the matron considers it madness to leap off a bridge fifteen stories high. Lynn grips the edge of the wooden platform, shaky for a moment.

"Five . . . four . . . three . . . two . . . one," the bungee master intones.

Lynn leans forward, bends her knees, and stretches her arms out in front of her. One more baby step sends her plummeting into the chasm.

Fighting the fall at first, Lynn lets go as she enters an aerial state of grace. All the life roles she has built—mother, professional, wife, community volunteer—are forgotten, her "inner house matron" silenced. Her body surrenders mid-arc and plunges peacefully toward the clear waters below. Unlike other jumpers before her whose arms were flailing wildly, Lynn's arms are outstretched perfectly. She feels, she will say later, like a bird.

She hits the end of the bungee cord and rebounds once, twice, then a third time, bobbing like a toy on an elastic string, then reaches for a pole extended to her by a man in a pickup raft. Lynn settles into the raft beaming. She feels a catharsis, arising from the loss of control so foreign to her. She is ecstatic. "This is what I wanted," she tells herself. The freedom from anxiety she is experiencing will linger for months.

A Messenger in Disguise. The Adventurer seeks—and finds—excitement and changes that give rise to new lifestyles and colorful adventures. Women guided by this archetype crave the catharsis of physical excitement and exploration. They often had little opportunity earlier in life to develop their athleticism or sense of adventure. Overcoming fear is a core goal.

The Adventurer can help a woman uproot a crippling anxiety, fear, or a shame that blocks her from connecting with her potential. This archetype often bears a second gift, the freedom to undertake some other personal mission. In Lynn's case, the New Zealand escapade helped her take difficult steps toward forging a second career in politics. For Sophia, whom we will meet later in this chapter, the Adventurer sparked a cross-country move and a period of intense spiritual and emotional growth.

This drive can transform the girls who were always picked last for playground teams into competitive rowers or cyclists as adults. It can make marathon runners of suburban matrons or drive computer programmers to abandon their office chairs in favor of a life on the trail or the road.

Adventurers are driving growth in new travel companies offering packages for the over-40 female. Menopausal Tours, an Internet travel company based in San Leandro, California, has seen a 15 percent increase in the past year in adventure-travel sign-ups among midlife women. Among their offerings: shooting the rapids on Chile's rugged Futaleufu River, riding hot-air balloons over the New Mexican desert, or jungle hiking on the Hawaiian isle of Molokai.

Three-fifths of the clients of Mountain Travel Sobek, Emeryville, California, specialists in small-group adventure travel to such destinations as Morocco and the Galápagos

Islands, are women whose average age is 49. Mountain Travel guides who work with women in their fifties see them blossoming and focusing anew on themselves.[1] One client, a former teacher, climbed Mount Kilimanjaro for the first time at 53. Her encore: running a marathon in Antarctica. Her goal is to run a marathon on every continent.

Women ages 45 through 59 are helping lead strong participation increases in rock-climbing, whitewater kayaking, and rafting. Racing Adventures, a Scottsdale, Arizona, auto-racing school, has seen a sharp increase in sign-ups by midlife women in just the past four years. Women now make up about 10 percent of the school's racing students, up from a handful twelve years ago; about four-fifths of those women students are over the age of 38.[2]

At the apex of the fitness craze—the triathlon—middle-aged women are posting gains on men. Women now comprise as much as 40 percent of the field in Ironman North America events, up from an estimated 20 percent five to ten years ago. From 40 to 50 percent of female participants in these grueling endurance contests are 30 to 44 years old, and significant numbers compete between the ages of 45 and 49.[3]

Half the members of Barb Odanaka's SkateboardMom.com website are over 40, and the number is growing fast. Hundreds have joined her multi-city "Mama Skate-O-Rama" tour doing grinds, ollies, and kick-flips alongside teenage skate park habitués. Skateboarding rivets women's attention to the present, says Odanaka, author of a book on skateboarding moms. "When you're zipping down a vertical wall, you have to be totally in the moment. You can't be thinking about whether Johnny has finished his homework. It's very Zen-like. If you aren't focused, you crash. It's that simple." Some of her friends, Odanaka adds, call skateboarding "Prozac on wheels."

The Adventurer's Power. Why would a 52-year-old woman undertake a seemingly pointless and almost overwhelmingly frightening bungee jump? The adrenaline rush, the ecstatic sense of freedom, the sheer craziness—all these Lynn invokes to explain her love of adventure. She quotes seventeenth-century philosopher Blaise Pascal's *"La coeur a ses raisons que la raison ne connaît point"*: The heart has reasons which reason does not know. "You can't overthink things. You've got to act. Thinking makes cowards of us all," she says. Heeding her "inner teenage boy" helped her drive the voice of reason into exile, just long enough to connect with deeper inner strengths.

The Adventurer sets aside ego concerns and other constraints to rediscover the importance of play at midlife. Play permits a person to give up self-importance without sacrificing self-esteem, Harvard University psychiatrist George Vaillant found in a fifty-year study of adult development.[4] Play allows experimentation with a new "self," a vision of who you want to become at midlife. And it makes midlife fun.

The Adventurer allows women to escape for a while from the losses of midlife. Bungee-jumping, motorcycle riding, rock-climbing, adventure travel, all allow us to dissociate from our pain. In fact, they force us to do so: The intense mental focus required by many sports, and the loss of control that adventures often entail, rip us away from our emptiness. In the process, we break old boundaries and learn about our limits and strengths.[5]

The Adventurer also transforms worries about declining physical capabilities and appearance into a positive drive for strength and fitness. This process, called sublimation, is a mature coping device, a way of turning a negative into a positive. And for many middle-aged women, appearance and weight become a discouraging preoccupation. Women worry more than men at this stage about their weight and body shape, and they tend to be far more critical of their appearance and negative in their own self-assessments. Well over half of women in their early fifties report their weight and figure are worse than five years earlier; over 10 percentage points more women than men give negative self-reports on these traits. This negativity partly reflects cultural pressures; women's actual weight gain by this life stage is in fact no greater than men's.[6] Nevertheless, the worries are real, and the Adventurer offers a way of sublimating them.

A Fiery Transition. Lynn's years spent raising her three children while working as a Washington, D.C., medical professional were "like being a short-order cook . . . a one-armed paperhanger on a windy day," she says. "It was a blur of cookies that I made, Halloween outfits we put together. I would fall asleep as if I were in a coma, before I even got into bed." Regarding herself in the mirror, Lynn feared she was becoming matronly, staid and sedate. Like other women in my study during their blackout years of work-and-family overload, Lynn sometimes had fantasies of getting in her car and driving away. And never coming back.

She began yearning for adventure. A friend told her about the thrill of bungee-jumping, and Lynn was intrigued. She also began dreaming of running for political office. "I said to myself, 'If I don't do this, ten years from now I'm going to turn around and say to myself, 'You fool, you had the chance and didn't take it.'"

The dreams became linked in Lynn's mind. As she planned a trip with her three teenagers to New Zealand, a center of bungee-jumping, she decided to take the leap. The lesson she learned there has changed the way she regards other ventures. "Bungee-jumping is a great metaphor for letting go of anxieties and taking the plunge into new areas. It's like being a spring filly again," she says. Once a decision is made, "you don't stop and think, 'What is the meaning of this?' and weigh the pros and cons. You just shut up and jump."

She returned home to lay the groundwork for running for public office, by moving with her family to a new community. It wasn't an easy decision. She and her husband loved their old house and hated to uproot the family. "It was like being stabbed in the stomach," she says. "That fiery transitional period, before you go into the next rebirth—it hurts so much."

But she has learned that the payoff warrants the pain. "Once you hit middle age, you have proven you do a lot of things—

hold a job, raise kids, be responsible. Now is a time to stretch ourselves again," she says.

Up next for Lynn: a 15-day hike to Everest Base Camp.

A Natural High. The role of Adventurer involves some risks, not the least of which is that you'll kill or permanently maim yourself.

Always the last person chosen for sports teams as a child, Sarah, a Tennessee physical therapist, plunged into kayaking and rowing as part of a Meltdown-style midlife crisis that began at age 49. "I loved that scary thrill that reminds me why it's so much fun to be alive," she says. "It's good to know I still have it in me to take risks."

Sarah paid a price for that self-knowledge. She broke her collarbone helping carry a heavy crew boat and can no longer lift with that shoulder.

But, "It was the physical activity that brought me to my knees—literally—and made me evaluate what I was truly looking for," she says. Her new clarity has led her to make new friends, begin attending concerts again, and swap her closetful of lookalike pants suits for flowing skirts rich in color and texture.

The Adventurer also can benefit from a more global, cosmopolitan view. Midlife crisis prompted Valerie, a corporate manager and mother from Connecticut, to hit the road, mostly by herself. "I have photographed summer sunsets at Stonehenge, driven the wrong way on the Rock of Gibraltar, been shaken down by Central European police, biked around the canals of Amsterdam, stood in awe at the wild colors of the Sistine Chapel, visited concentration camps in Poland," she says. Back home, she decided to test her mettle in a new, more altruistic way: She is training to become a Red Cross disaster response worker.

The Adventurer can also set off a pressure-release valve. Alyson, an Oregon attorney with three school-age children, verged on despair as she approached 40. She felt stifled by the prospect of continuing her juggling act for the years still needed to finish raising her children. But she did not want to do anything potentially destructive to her family.

Her newfound love of running marathons surprised even Alyson. "I never considered myself an athlete," she says. "I never thought I could run. If you stood behind me with a loaded gun I wouldn't run."

But her restlessness had led her to begin running a bit with her husband, and she was pleased one day to hit six miles. At a friend's house that night, over wine after dinner, Alyson threw out a challenge: "Let's run a marathon!" Her friend quickly agreed. "For both of us, it was such a challenge and such a goal. I wanted to feel like, 'I can still do that!'" They picked an Arizona marathon four months hence and began a rigorous training regimen.

Crossing the finish line in her first race was "probably the most natural high I ever had, next to having my babies," Alyson says. She ran six marathons in the ensuing eighteen months, qualifying for and finishing the Boston Marathon. Her best time: 3:39, a major accomplishment for a 44-year-old runner. Alyson has also built a close group of like-minded friends, six women in their forties who meet daily at 5:15 A.M. for a training run.

The Adventurer has proven the perfect archetype for Alyson's

Moderate midlife crisis. Middle age "would be a lot harder if I weren't a runner," she says. And it has given her courage to dream again.

Up next for Alyson: adventure travel. "I'd love to do a trek in Nepal, or one of those cool river-rafting trips."

Into the West. For Sophia, one of those cool river-rafting trips touched off a Sonic Boom. The midwestern mother of three was in her 40s when she signed on to run the Colorado River rapids with an adventure tour service. The connection she forged with the natural world on this trip would come to signify far more, ushering in an overhaul of her personal, professional, and spiritual life. Her story highlights the potential of adventure as a catalyst for broader change.

For years Sophia had tried to calm a mounting midlife restlessness. As a child she had been a tomboy, but in her teens she assumed the prim demeanor expected of girls in her upper-middle-class community. In high school she strived for perfection and was voted top citizenship honors. For twenty years she cared lovingly for her husband and daughters. A hardworking editor, she switched to a higher-paying corporate job in her late thirties, to help put her girls through college. She did not like the work. Her boss was rude and at times verbally abused her. Her entire paycheck was consumed by college and household expenses.

As Sophia entered her forties and the empty-nest stage, she began questioning all the values that had guided her. At her twenty-fifth high school reunion, a group of her women friends gathered to tell their stories. "Do you want the white-picket fence story, or do you want to know how it really was?" one woman began. She proceeded to relate a story of the alcoholism and near-bankruptcy that secretly bedeviled a family that had always maintained a picture-perfect image. At a church retreat for women, Sophia heard similar stories of marital and family discord. She came away shaken.

"Here were all these people acting as if everything is wonderful, as if nothing is wrong. And it's not true. Everything seemed a facade to me after that."

Sophia recalls standing at her stove one evening cooking dinner for her husband, who was watching TV in the living room. Out of nowhere came the thought "Omigod, is this the rest of my life? I don't want to spend the years I have left preparing dinner for someone who comes home and sits on the couch clicking the remote."

She increasingly felt drained, and began for the first time to experience health problems, including stress-related abdominal pain and a respiratory infection that forced a brief hospital stay. "The well is dry," she thought. "I can't give any more. I'm empty. I am falling apart."

The river-rafting tour was an attempt to reignite her inner spark. It did much more. At the end of an eight-hour day on the water, Sophia accepted a dinner invitation from a friend of her rafting guide, a man who had built an expansive western home in the rugged terrain near the river. "I walked through his house and out into his garden, and my soul came back. I remembered who I was, the woman I had given up," Sophia says.

Sophia never intended to end her marriage; she had been faithful and loyal for twenty years to her husband. But as Sophia's midlife crisis became too much for either partner to handle within the confines of marriage, it fell apart. She and the man she had met had a brief affair, backpacking through the Rockies, opening a new world to Sophia. "He was like an angel, awakening my love for the West," she says.

They broke up after Sophia realized he was not what he had seemed, that she had projected larger-than-life qualities onto him. But "I later thanked him for shocking me and being the impetus" to overhaul her life, she says.

She started her own consulting business to gain control over her hours, and moved to the West, where camping, hiking, rafting, and being outdoors took on a permanent and central role in her life. Her life expanded in several directions. She took up meditation and pored over an eclectic variety of readings from many spiritual traditions. "I pick and choose from the various philosophies that are out there," she says.

She has learned much about herself. "I have a great connection to the earth. It's very important for me to be in Nature." It is essential to feeling alive and to growing in her relationships and in her spiritual life, Sophia says.

And she is seeing the world. She has hiked in South America and Europe and meditated at Stonehenge. Also, in a pattern typical of many women in my study, she has engaged in a series of relationships with men, each one better than the last.

All her work on herself has healed Sophia, body and soul. Although she worries about the impact of her divorce on her children, her relationships with each of them have improved, and they enjoy traveling with Sophia. After decades of self-sacrifice for others, her midlife crisis has "helped me understand that if you choose for yourself," she says, "everybody else is happy."

4

✦ ✦ ✦

THE LOVER

Break my heart, so love can flow more freely.

— SUFI PROVERB

At the peak of a brilliant career in her late forties, Carly faced a problem she could not solve.

The California executive had amassed plenty of clout in the workplace. She had launched products and helped engineer turnarounds at both blue chip companies and fast-growing start-ups. She had founded her own successful company.

In her personal life, however, she was paralyzed by fear. After nearly twenty years, her marriage was on the rocks after three separations and failed reconciliations. Her husband had withdrawn from her; they had not made love in years. He had undermined her trust by mismanaging financial matters. Although Carly and her husband sought counseling, divorce seemed inevitable.

But Carly was afraid of the financial consequences, and even more, of being alone. In her unhappiness, she had gained weight and felt colorless and dull. She believed she would never find another man to love her. She felt herself skidding toward an emotional breakdown.

Sifting through her belongings one day, she opened a little-used storage compartment in the headboard of her bed. There lay a diary, its paper cover marbleized with age, that she had written as a young woman before her marriage. Carly opened the little book, and from its pages emerged a woman she had forgotten—an attractive, vibrant, fun-loving female with "lots of men swirling around me, interesting men from all different walks of life. I was having fun. It was really very powerful," she says. "I wondered, 'Where did this woman go?' I liked her." It was a side of herself she had buried, the sensual feminine side, to compete in the executive suite and to survive a sexless marriage.

Thus began Carly's seven-year odyssey in the Lover role. Facing her demons in a Moderate-mode midlife crisis, "I rediscovered a 'me' I had buried," she says. She began a series of new relationships. She gained resounding affirmation that she could not only still attract men, but much younger men. She even survived a couple of major-league heartbreaks.

Ultimately, she found a love so mature, so satisfying, that it transcended any relationship she had hoped for.

A Complex Archetype. The Lover seeks intimacy, love, or sexual fulfillment at midlife. A powerful and potentially destructive archetype, it is driving the rise in the number of midlife women having extramarital affairs, filing for divorce, and dating younger men.

The Lover derives its psychological power partly from women's new sense of freedom at midlife. Many experience the loss of fertility at menopause as a gain in sexual liberty. The empty nest releases others from bonds to home and hearth. These freedoms enable many women to approach a developmental milestone they have not yet passed—the attainment of mature adult love, or intimacy, a building block for psychological health and well-being.

Some women in my study who were drawn to the Lover role achieved more fulfilling relationships. Some revitalized their marriages, finding deeper intimacy with their spouses. For some, as in Lainey's story in this chapter, the Lover ushered in a season of "young love" for the first time.

For still others, the Lover served as a catalyst, sparking needed changes in other areas of life. In these midlife crises, the Lover acted like a fuse to some buried psychic dynamite, creating so much destruction that women were forced to make changes in other realms. Naomi's story in this chapter illustrates this pattern.

The Lover has a dark side. Sometimes it distracts women who really should be working on revitalizing other areas of their lives, such as career or spiritual pursuits. It can destroy marriages that deserve to be saved. It can be a trickster, luring a woman into misbegotten relationships that look like an improvement on old ones, but in fact repeat the mistakes of the past. A woman's quest for intimacy can become frenetic, pulling her down into promiscuity. Also, what feels like passion is sometimes just a craving to prove you are still physically attractive.

The Lover can be a Trojan horse, introducing an army of troubles a woman is not yet ready to handle. The consequences can trap a woman in a netherworld, pained by the damage she has done with no chance of escape.

The Lover also has a nonromantic side. As intimacy becomes a top priority at midlife, many women simply seek deeper friendships. In sharing and trust, women find in these relationships the freedom to be themselves, relax, and be open and experiment with new ways of being. Like time spent with a lover, this nonsexual intimacy allows women to be completely truthful, to shed the concerns of ego and self-image, and to face midlife turbulence squarely.[1]

Recalling the Forgotten. Finding the diary helped propel Carly through the pain of divorce and face her fear, that she would be alone for the rest of her life. Motivated by the reemergence of her sensual, feminine side, she mustered the courage to start dating.

It was rough sledding at first. She had a consuming affair with an investment banker she met on a plane. He showered Carly with a diamond ring and other gifts. "We had a great romance," Carly says. "It was intense and very ardent."

Until it wasn't. The investment banker abruptly dropped out of sight while away on a European business trip, sending Carly into a panic. When he finally answered his phone, she cried, "I've been trying to reach you for days!"

His response was brusque and unkind: "I can't go on this way.

This is too much." Devastated, Carly would later learn that the investment banker had lied to her, claiming he was divorced when he was not. Looking at the ring he had given her, Carly wondered if the diamonds were false, too. "I realized I wouldn't know a real diamond from a fake one"—or a real commitment from a pretense. It was a rough initiation into the world of midlife love.

Picking up the pieces, Carly slimmed down and lightened her hair. She began dating a younger man, a software engineer ten years her junior, who decided he did not want to become a stepfather to Carly's two school-age children.

It was her children who suggested a change of course. "Mom, why don't you date someone your own age?" they kidded her, and presented some candidates they had found online and deemed worthy. Intrigued, Carly decided to have some fun posting her own profile. She donned a little black dress for a portrait, wrote a lively (and accurate) description of herself as an adventurous fun lover and posted it on several sites. Her image—a vibrant, hazel-eyed woman with a warm smile and shoulder-length blond hair—drew immediate attention.

Within hours, she was deluged by responses, some from "stunningly handsome" men as much as twenty years younger. Carly was incredulous; she had been honest about her age on the websites. Not only did it seem to make no difference to younger men who replied—it almost seemed like a draw.

All the male attention was a tremendous confidence builder for Carly. "Here I was, a formerly semi-dowdy executive mother, and what some of these men did to try to get my attention was amazing," she says. Her romantic adventures became a hot topic among her friends. Some of the men sent provocative photos while others wrote erotic messages. Two were so eloquent that she responded in kind.

"I had never seen this side of myself before," Carly says. "I have a lot of playfulness, a lot of sexuality in me." At 48, she had learned something new about herself: "Sex is a central part of life. It's important to me."

Carly dated dozens of guys in the ensuing years—a model for *GQ* magazine ("He was pretty emotionally remote. We just had one date," she says); several handsome men in their twenties ("I really liked their energy"); and an athletic, youthful 54-year-old construction executive ("I fell head over heels"). She decided to end her online adventures after the construction executive abruptly revealed he was dating someone else. "I was so mad," Carly says. "I decided, I'm tired of this bouncing around. It's time to get a little more serious."

She agreed to a blind date arranged by a friend, with an older man, a blond, lanky information-security consultant. He had little in common with the dark, muscular men who usually attracted her; there was little chemistry between them at first. But Carly was ready to look deeper. She hosted the consultant and a group of friends at a dinner party, and was charmed when he sent her a gift basket the next day.

His kindness "shocked me," Carly says. "He treats me like a queen. And he adores my children." They exchanged a series of e-mails resembling an old-fashioned correspondence, sharing thoughts on music and art. "This guy has gravitas," Carly realized. Her lover spent hours one day waiting patiently for her at an airport—something no man had ever done. The relationship has blossomed into something different from any she has ever had—deeper, more patient, more respectful.

Slowly, she is opening the door to greater intimacy. While Carly still has her own house, kids, and career, she is learning to let her lover extend emotional support—to take care of her, in some ways. "My husband never did that," she says. She also is taking more time for herself, curbing her work hours, eating healthy, and working out three to five times a week.

Her seven-year midlife crisis seems to be nearing a satisfying end. "I feel more like a total person, in my work life, my family life, and my social and sexual life, than ever before," Carly says.

May Meets December. Carly's lively love life reflects a sharp reversal of traditional dating and mating roles. In the past, it was men who sought out younger mates while their former partners pined away at home. But now, affairs between younger men and midlife women are increasingly common. Some younger men are looking for an experienced sex partner who will not pressure them to marry or start a family. Others feel older women appreciate them more than do women their own age.

For a woman at midlife, the rewards are clear: affirmation that she is attractive, for one. This need, so prevalent among midlife women that it amounts to an epidemic, is the number one reason women have extramarital affairs, says Janet Lever, a sexuality researcher at the University of California at Los Angeles. Women seek affirmation because "society is instilling doubts about their attractiveness," Lever says. Women's insecurities on this front surface over and over in research, shaping behavior from hormone usage to sexual satisfaction. The MacArthur Foundation "Midlife in the United States" study found fully three-fifths of women in their forties and fifties worry about losing their physical appeal.[2]

Also, many midlife women simply enjoy a romp with a vital, virile male. Many women in my study had trouble finding men their age with matching energy and interest in sex. "Men in their fifties often have a mind-set that they've already done everything, that they're in a decline, or a deceleration of their lives," Carly says. "That wasn't my mind-set at all, and I don't just mean sexually. Their whole outlook on life was different. I liked the energy of the younger men. That's how I saw myself."

Defying old cultural norms, a satisfying sexual relationship is almost as important to today's midlife women as to men that age. Two-thirds of midlife women ages 45 to 59 cite sex as important to their quality of life, nearly as many as the three-fourths of midlife men who value it highly, says a 1999 study by the AARP. More than half of women in this age group still feel sexual desire at least once a week, some as often as daily.[3]

Many women actually become more able to experience orgasm as they near the age of 40.[4] And recent research suggests that midlife is the first time many women feel free to focus on themselves and their own enjoyment during sex, rather than on their partners. Typically, they have left behind the pressures of youth, including child care, fear of unwanted pregnancy, or damage to their reputation.

As Carly's story shows, these freedoms set the stage for tremendous growth in the sexual and emotional arenas. "Popular belief holds that once humans reach physical maturity, sexual development stops. Nothing could be further from the truth," maintains Thomasina Sharpe, an assistant professor in the medical school at the University of South Alabama, Mobile. Instead, sexual development is "an ongoing process of recognizing, accepting, and expressing one's self as a sexual being."[5]

Like Carly, Lainey took giant steps at midlife in her growth toward full womanhood—from a sharply different starting point.

First Love at Fifty. Lainey's midlife crisis began in her early forties, in a highly unusual way: She decided to become celibate.

A history of bad relationships had left the Washington, D.C., communications specialist too discouraged to keep trying. She kept picking men who made her feel insecure, afraid of abandonment, and dependent—despite the fact that she had been supporting herself nicely for decades as a single professional woman.

"I'm taking myself out of the dating game," she vowed. "I'm going to be celibate for as long as it takes me to figure out why I haven't found a healthy relationship."

In a measured midlife crisis in the Moderate mode, Lainey set about overhauling her life. She switched to a job at a different company where, for the first time in years, she had a boss who encouraged her to grow professionally. She had her customary blond pageboy trimmed to a more youthful pixie cut that accentuated her beautiful eyes and warm smile. She sold her tiny apartment and bought a two-bedroom place with room for guests.

For her bedroom, she bought a pair of antique lamps. "I put one on each side of the bed and thought, 'Maybe one day there will be someone else in this bed with me.' I just couldn't give up hope. I had to believe, for myself, that I would not be alone forever."

She also entered therapy. "I said to myself, 'I'm smart. I'm successful. What's going on here? If I don't address these problems now, when am I going to do it? I need to be brave and figure out what makes me tick, and what hangs me up.'"

Her therapist helped her see that she had been stuck too long in the emotional orientation she had learned from her mother. As a child, she had never felt secure or accepted. Keeping her weight down was a battle for Lainey, and she had always felt she disappointed her mother, a slender, elegant fashionista. "I was never right, I never looked right, nothing fit," she says. Although Lainey had long since moved away from her mother and established her independence, she continued to pick as dates men who re-created that emotional predicament, men who were critical and inconstant. It was time, Lainey realized, to forge her own, authentic identity. She also began taking medication for minor depression.

Two events accelerated Lainey's transformation. She was thrust face-to-face with her own mortality by the September 11 terrorist attacks, which killed or hurt many people she knew. And just two weeks later, her mother had a disabling stroke.

Finding joy in life assumed new urgency for Lainey. To feed an old passion for music, she bought a new sound system and rearranged her living room to give herself room to dance. She started going to concerts and rekindled an old interest in the Allman Brothers Band. It was on the band's website that Lainey first encountered John, another fan.

"He was a man of few words, but his words were funny, droll," Lainey says. Exchanging e-mails, Lainey learned John, a musician-turned-teacher, lived in the South and had an adult daughter on the East Coast. In the past, she never would have had the courage to take the next step. But the "now-or-never" mind-set of midlife crisis emboldened her. Seeing a particularly salient e-mail by John, she tapped out a response with the word *sexy* as the subject line.

"John, I just have to tell you: I think you have an incredibly sexy intellect," she wrote. "I know you've been trying to date and haven't met the right person. But I hope someday you meet the right woman, someone who realizes what a great person you are."

His reply terrified her. He would be in the Washington area over the holidays. Would Lainey like to go out for a drink?

Seated at her computer, she blushed and panicked. "No! No! No!" was her first impulse. Then Lainey's new, what-the-hell side kicked in: "Why not?" Their e-mails flowed more steadily.

Both loved the youthful memories the Allman Brothers evoked; John was a musician himself. "If the things that made you so happy when you were an idealistic teenager still make you happy, and they're still out there, well hey, why not? Why not go for it?" Lainey says they agreed.

When John arrived in Washington over the holidays and called Lainey for the first time, "I felt like I wanted to fall into his voice" on the phone, she says. His refined baritone, with a slight accent, "had that southern courtliness I have always found sexy." That evening, they sat elbow-to-elbow in a booth at a blues bar and talked over dinner.

They kidded each other about being "virgins." Each had been out of the dating scene for some time—John for six years, and Lainey for nine. "It was like a first love," she says. They went back to Lainey's apartment and John waited for her to make the first move before making love—a courtesy that, after a youth and young adulthood spent warding off men's advances, she found empowering. A small voice in the back of Lainey's head intoned, "He's for me"—knowledge, she says, from "an inner, inspired place."

After two nights together, they agreed they were crazy about each other. "I feel like you are the high school boyfriend I never had," Lainey told him. Old songs from her teens, "Cherish" and "Never My Love," drifted back to mind. Back then, such songs "filled me with unbearable longing and despair, that those romantic wishes would never be fulfilled," Lainey says. But now, "I am filled with absolute joy" on hearing them. "This really feels like young love, but with a mature mind."

For Lainey, that means enjoying both sex and friendship with the same man. Making love for Lainey and John is a ritual with sacred overtones. They light candles, play music, and shower together afterward, taking time to luxuriate in each other. Her old self-consciousness in bed is gone. She tells John what she wants and does not want.

And both of her antique bedside lamps are getting full-time use at last. Less than two years after they met, Lainey and John got married.

Reality Check. Beyond delightful tales like Lainey's, the dark side of the Lover can be misleading. A woman in the Lover role may be so eager to find what she needs that she believes she actually sees those qualities in a partner—when they are not there. Such projections can distort our perceptions not only of lovers, but of leaders or public figures we admire. This wishful thinking can be a route to personal growth, but it always takes the hard way. It lures women into affairs with partners who cannot give them what they need.

The example of Molly, a consultant from California, is particularly clear-cut. In her case, the long illness and death of her partner of twenty years ended a sexual dry spell and sparked a midlife crisis. At 41, she began a torrid transcontinental affair with a former high school sweetheart. In an outpouring of pent-up passion, Molly wrote poetry and rejoiced in their lovemaking. "I felt like I was eighteen again," she says.

But as time tore away veils of illusion, Molly began to see that her lover was not who she thought he was: she could not depend on him and they were generally incompatible. Deeply in pain, she broke it off. It was not until years later that she and her former lover, meeting as friends, could talk about how each had projected onto the other the qualities they had wanted to see, rather than the ones that were there.

Family and friends are often baffled by the odd suitors who crop up in the lives of women blinded by projection. Several women in my study tumbled into affairs with men who seemed irresistible, only to discover later that they were utter jerks. Waking up next to a stranger, regarding their partner in the harsh light of truth, they wonder what he did with the man of their dreams.

Mismatched relationships are a hallmark of midlife crisis. Examples from my study abound. A computer programmer takes up with an unemployed alcoholic; a corporate CEO tumbles into bed with a tour guide; a manager develops a blinding crush on her piano teacher. The prognosis for these odd match-ups is dim. Nothing in matters of the heart is impossible, of course. But in not one single case in my study did such awkward pairings mature into lasting love.

Lovers also can indulge in compulsive behavior. A woman's desire to be seen as sexually attractive can run amok, pushing her over the edge into an eating or exercise disorder. I am reminded of this hazard every time I visit my own health club. We women in our forties and fifties dance a fitness-obsessed pas de deux with our teenage and twenty-something counterparts. We wear the same tight workout garb, the same blond highlights in our hair. We cycle politely together through the same rows of exercise machines. Our muscles stretch down the same lean, hard-toned legs. Those of us in middle age display a few more wrinkles, more papery skin, a little more strain. But we march to the same inner drummer, the same perfectionist mantra, as our daughters.

Our obsessions are often most obvious when we see them reflected in others. In an encounter on the TV series *Sex and the City*, the alluringly dressed heroine Carrie and her friends, all in their thirties, confront a group of rich teenage girls in equally sexy garb. "Are they trying to look like us?" Carrie wonders aloud. "Or are we trying to look like them?"

In the heat of midlife crisis, as Naomi's story shows, a preoccupation with appearance can easily cross the line into the slow self-starvation of an eating or exercise disorder.

The Look of Heartbreak. "Do you want to know what heartbreak looks like? This is what heartbreak looks like!" Naomi shrieks in an interview, mimicking Diane Keaton in her romance with Jack Nicholson in that movie ode to midlife love, *Something's Gotta Give*.

But unlike Keaton's character, Naomi is not in love with a sagging 63-year-old. This 40-year-old married mother of two, regarded by her friends as Supermom, has fallen hard for her personal trainer—tall, dark, built, and fourteen years younger. Her agonized lament marks the end of a year-long affair that to Naomi has been the greatest love of her life—a love that touched off a midlife crisis in the classic Sonic Boom mode.

Middle-aged women developing the hots for their personal trainers have become a cultural cliché. But Naomi's experience was anything but trite. For her, a psychologist who had left her career to raise her two children, Ty represented freedom, flamboyance, adventure, easy sociability. He afforded a diversion from a marriage she found boring and a child-rearing routine that, despite her deep love for her children, forced her into a lifestyle she had never wanted. The affair also pressured Naomi to grow, by blasting her life so far off her old track that she had to begin asking, and answering, some tough questions about herself.

Some deep crosscurrents in Naomi's childhood roiled up in a tidal wave at midlife. As a child, she loved spontaneity. In her teens, she dreamed of being a dancer—"I thought I would go to New York and have lots of affairs and never get married."

She adored her father, a flamboyant, charming, but irresponsible man who alternately fascinated and disappointed her. "My father was a man who said, 'This is a great big world. Go out and seize it and see it and be free,'" she says. His warmth enabled him to make friends anywhere.

On the other hand, her father's wanderings made him unavailable most of the time to his family, and Naomi grew up with an unmet yen for security. Naomi's father and mother were divorced, and neither wanted to raise Naomi and her brother. The children bounced from house to house, living with relatives and friends. To learn about love, Naomi watched TV and movies, feeding on the celluloid passions of Hollywood lovers and the melodrama of soap operas.

When Naomi grew into adulthood and made the marriage

decision, she opted for security. In her husband, who is ten years older, she saw what she had lacked as a child: a kind, responsible, caring partner. "He is a wonderful man, but not the love of my life. I married him for security," Naomi says. "You need a yin and a yang. I was the one making friends, and he was the steadying force. He was stable, he worked hard, he loves to be with family. Of course you're going to marry that kind of man."

But her husband also tended to control their lives together, and Naomi made compromise after compromise in the years that followed. He wanted two children. She did not. He wanted a big house in the suburbs. She did not. He prevailed, and Naomi dropped out of the workforce for a decade, quitting her job to stay home with their two kids in the suburbs. Setting aside her dreams, Naomi strived mightily to be a better parent than she had had, and succeeded beyond anyone's expectations. She nursed each of her children for a year, refused to hire sitters, made her own baby food. Her family kidded her about how Naomi the Wanderer had morphed into Naomi the Earth Mother.

"I was out to prove that children mattered, that children could be first in their parents' lives," she says. "It never occurred to me in my wildest dreams that I would have an affair."

But unfortunately, she ignored herself and her needs. Somewhere along the way, so gradually that she barely noticed, Naomi stopped doing all the things she loved—her therapist would later say she stopped living her own life. The last time she could remember experiencing any vitality or excitement was when she backpacked through Europe early in her marriage,

while her husband did a stint working there. Beneath consciousness, her sacrifices quietly mounted to smothering proportions.

Naomi first noticed Ty during her regular workouts at her gym;
tall, handsome, and charming, he was hard to miss. Petite and dark,
with boundless energy, Naomi looked far younger than her forty
years. When Ty began hanging around during her regular workouts, then pursuing her for conversation, she was "swept away.
This man wanted to know what I needed and wanted. I came home
and made a list. It was almost like he had peeked inside my head,"
Naomi says. "Ty embodied passion, excitement, romance. I have
never felt that way before." She was secretly delighted, too, that at
age 40 she could still attract a man in his twenties.

They began taking walks together and seeing each other on
weekends. She baked him bread. He told her he was "head over
heels" in love with her.

Naomi told Ty her love for him was so intense that "no one
else will ever feel this way about you."

They continued for months to meet alone at times when
Naomi's husband and kids were away, flirting with talk of choco-
late martinis, whipped cream, hot tubs, and sex. Their trysts
remained only talk. They never had intercourse, limiting themselves to kisses and caresses in what Naomi calls "an emotional
affair." But the chemistry between them was transformative to
Naomi. She jettisoned her baggy suburban-mom wardrobe for
sleek jeans, dangly jewelry, sexy sandals, and tank tops that fit
like a second skin; she could pass for 30 at any hip New York bar.
"The before-Ty clothing is all gone," she says.

The relationship also brought dark echoes of her past. Like Naomi's father, Ty could make friends anywhere. He knew all the best bars, could greet the bartenders by name. He was Peter Pan, stuck in perpetual youth, living with his mother, taking occasional house-sitting jobs, ceaselessly dodging commitment. Naomi saw it differently: "His lifestyle represented freedom," she says.

Their relationship was not always so sunny. Ty verged at times on verbally abusing her. When she once asked him to turn down his booming music, he chided, "What's the matter? Are you getting old?" He would draw her close, then push her away for days. "It's almost as if he needs me in his orbit, but when he gets close he gets scared," she says. With her life rocketing out of control, the destructive side of the Lover emerged. Naomi clamped down hard on her eating and her weight dropped like a rock. Ten pounds down from her once-healthy weight, she began to look emaciated.

Finally, Ty told her he was seeing other women. "This is too much work for me. It's too hard," he said.

Naomi felt as if someone had punched her in the stomach. "I am so worth it!" she told him angrily. "Isn't this what relationships are all about?"

The loss sent Naomi into a free fall. "The brightest thing in my life, other than my kids, has walked out of my world and isn't coming back," she told herself. Devastated, she burst into tears while volunteering at her children's school. Friends insisted she get counseling.

For Naomi, the relationship was a catalyst for some hard work on herself. One reason she was so attracted to Ty, she realizes now, is that "I had stopped living for such a long, long time. I had stopped doing all the things I loved." Slowly, a new path began to emerge for Naomi. "You haven't nourished yourself in six years," her therapist told her. "You seem to have lost your sense of self. You need to find more passion in things that are for you." With the therapist's help, Naomi cut herself off from Ty, curbed her workouts, and started eating again.

Then, the therapist began at the beginning: "Let's figure out why you're so sad," and encouraged her to explore why she had been so susceptible to Ty's charms. The therapist helped her revive an old passion for painting. Naomi took satisfaction in entering a couple of local shows, where her work was well received. Her therapist also encouraged her to begin working part-time again, at a community nonprofit where she widened her network of friends and enjoyed working with children. Both pursuits are helping Naomi practice savoring life—her own life—again.

Her marriage is another story. Naomi's husband knew she was smitten with Ty, and he is angry. But both he and Naomi want to provide a secure home for their children. And Naomi is not ready to leave. "If I'm going to leave my marriage, I'm going to leave it for me," and not because of an affair, she says. Before making any decision, she knows she needs to figure out why her life took such a dramatic and painful turn.

Naomi's story illustrates one aspect of the Lover's trickster side.

Because many women's midlife affairs reach so deep to unmet needs, because they are so electrifying, they can blind women to the real purpose they serve—to divert them from a lifestyle they no longer want but are too fearful or confused to change.

Naomi's missteps are crystal clear, in hindsight. "I wish I'd had enough confidence when I was thirty-two to look at my life and say, 'First, you're not happy, get out of this marriage, and second, go do what you want to do,'" Naomi says. "Why didn't I become a dancer on Broadway when I was twenty-two? Women should go out and have the time of their lives. And make sure when you make choices, they're your choices."

Hindsight has also helped her see Ty's unkindnesses, including his habit of flirting with numerous women. Yet she holds on to the belief that with her Ty crossed a line, into a love too deep for a Peter Pan to sustain. Her belief has left her with some fundamental questions about relationships.

"I look at all my friends who have these great partners. I started asking people, 'Is this the love of your life? What does that mean to you?'" she says.

One friend replied, "Naomi, you don't need passion in your life. You have someone who can take care of you," meaning her husband.

"Have you ever felt passion?" Naomi asked her.

"No, it's too scary," her friend said.

At that moment, a gulf opened between them. "I never would have given this relationship up for the world," Naomi told her. "It was the best feeling of my life."

A Cocoon of Bliss. Even the most passionate and delightful affairs can bring consequences one is not ready to face, however. Emma's turmoil began in her late forties with the death of her mother. As a small child, Emma had been turned over by her mother to her grandparents to be raised. Although she saw her mother from time to time, Emma never healed from what felt to her like abandonment. Unmet needs rose to the surface. "I didn't ask my mother questions I should have asked her, and now it's too late," she says.

Emma worked hard to overcome that loss, marrying in her early twenties to a hardworking, reliable man and building a stable home life. It was a choice made not out of passion but out of a desire for security; living with her husband, Emma says, was like living with her brother. She built a career in California pharmaceutical sales, cultivated an image as a strong, independent businesswoman, and immersed herself in raising her three kids and heading the PTA. On the outside, she was a modern female success story. But on the inside, "I always felt like the little child with her nose pressed up against the window, looking at everybody else being happy," she says.

The Lover's emergence at midlife forced her to close that distance with others. For years, she had a recurring nighttime dream of being enmeshed in joyful lovemaking with a soul mate, evoking a passion she had never felt in her marriage. "My lover in the dream never had a face," she says. Nevertheless, the fantasy "was so great that sometimes I wished I wouldn't wake up."

At midlife, the dream took center stage. Her mother's death, coupled with her children's departure for college, pushed Emma to the edge. She was overwhelmed by an abiding sense of emptiness. "I looked at myself for the first time in twenty-five years and realized there was not a lot of time left," she says. "I was overcome by the most powerful desire to make sure I didn't die unfulfilled." She could no longer bear to watch TV love stories because they aroused such a deep yearning. "I needed to make sure that I knew what it felt like to really be loved, and to love. I thought about it all the time." Her success in business gave her the confidence to hope for more.

Then, in a chance encounter, the man of her dreams acquired a face. In a public lobby she bumped into Dan, a married friend and businessman in her town. "He hugged me and we stood there holding hands. And it just flashed into my mind, that he was that person, that face in my dreams," Emma says. She had not seen Dan for a few weeks. "Where have you been?" she asked.

"Well, do you want to have lunch tomorrow, and we can talk about it?" he asked.

Over lunch, Dan told her he had been avoiding her because he felt he was falling in love with her. Thus began a secret affair that would last six years. Dan proved a warm, kind, expressive lover, so secure in his manhood and so attuned to his feelings that being intimate came easily. He loved to go dancing, to hear music, to travel. He loved Emma's oil paintings, the landscapes and nature scenes she had begun doing after her children left home. And most of all, he loved Emma.

They arranged secret rendezvous on business trips. They

basked in candlelit hot tubs, in body rubs with massage oil, in long, passionate lovemaking. At age 50, Emma knew intimacy at last. "I was in a cocoon of total bliss, emotionally and sexually," she says. "I had the most fabulous time. It was the happiest period of my life." She moved out of her house and, at Dan's urging, filed for divorce.

It was at that point that Emma's midlife crisis began the Flameout trajectory. Old fears surfaced, and soon she began feeling she had made a mistake. She dreaded losing "the only family I had ever known," she says. Also looming was the prospect of becoming stepmother to Dan's children—a role she did not want. She panicked, left Dan, and tried to go home again.

Emma yearned to apply to her marriage what she had learned from Dan. "I had learned how to love. I had changed dramatically," she says. "I was so willing, I wanted so desperately, to give love to my husband. I felt a huge responsibility for the lack of intimacy and love in our marriage. Because I had found it, because I had had it, I thought I could give it. And I thought if I gave it, it would come back."

But sadly, it was too late. Emma returned to a home that was no longer there. The damage was beyond repair. Her husband could not forgive her for leaving. He, too, had secretly begun another relationship during her absence. Although he ended that affair, their marriage has never recovered. Her husband has refused counseling, and he and Emma have never achieved the intimacy Emma hoped for.

Looking back, Emma sometimes wishes she had married

Dan, who is now remarried. But moving away from her husband left her feeling so much like an abandoned child, she says, that "I simply could not do that then." Emma has decided to stay in her marriage; urgent extended-family needs are keeping her busy.

Regrets aside, having her midlife crisis was better than no change at all, she says. "While life has not turned out the way I had hoped, I am satisfied to live with the decisions I made. I certainly will not die unfulfilled, as I dreaded," Emma says. "I now have many exciting stories to tell my blue-haired friends as we reminisce at night around the fireplace in the old folks' home."

Hazards Ahead. If I could install a flaming yellow CAUTION light to warn married readers of this chapter, I would. The Lover can act as a delightful archetype, fostering rich personal growth. The Lover can deliver a bracing wake-up call to couples who need a sexual revival. The Lover can also pound the last nail into the coffin of a hopelessly repressive or abusive marriage, giving a woman needed energy to escape.

Too often, however, salvageable marriages that probably should be saved are dashed on the rocks of midlife crises. Marriage in the last half of life, or any time, should not be cast aside if there is any chance it can grow and change to accommodate a woman's needs. Marriage is linked to many measures of psychological well-being, including lower distress, higher self-esteem, and a deeper sense of purpose. Many of the women in my study found it easy in the throes of midlife crisis to forget all that. Too often, those who fail to find the right balance—to gain control of a new relationship, as Odysseus did with Circe, rather than succumbing thoughtlessly to impulsive desires—do irreparable damage to their marriages, damage they later regret.

Understanding two more characteristics of the Lover can avert this mistake. First, this archetype is so powerful that it is easy to overreact. Like an infatuated teenager, a woman in midlife crisis may be so swept away by joy and passion that she jumps to a new partner—only to discover she has repeated the same mistake she made when she chose her spouse. The new lover is just the same old problem in a different wrapper. These women have failed to do the hard work needed to grow before making a new commitment.

Second, the Lover can be deceitfully seductive. It can trick a woman into scapegoating her spouse for problems that are actually of her own making. Western culture places so much emphasis on romantic love that it is easy to kid yourself into believing a new lover will solve all your problems. Too many women blame their marriages for midlife distress, rather than facing the true cause of their stagnation: their own failure to seize new experiences, nurture their talents, and do the hard searching needed to find meaning in life.

"Some women complain about their husbands, when the real issue is that they themselves have failed to grow," says Washington, D.C., psychiatrist Lise Van Susteren. "They're sitting there with nothing to do, and they think it's their husband's fault. The poor bastard walks in and has no idea he's in trouble.

"A woman like this may think she's going to go out and find another love," Van Susteren says. "I want to ask, 'Exactly what is it you're planning to offer a new lover, besides sitting around and reading the newspaper?'"

In the long run, other archetypes may hold better answers for restless women at midlife.

5

✦ ✦ ✦

THE LEADER

Well-behaved women rarely make history.

—LAUREL THATCHER ULRICH, HISTORIAN

The life Leanne had built for herself by age 38 seemed a shaky foundation for entrepreneurial success. The Colorado mother had hit bottom after a divorce. Her ex-husband had moved across the continent with their children, her father had died, and anxiety had sent her weight into a tailspin.

Once a top law school student, she was reduced to working as a temp, filing and clerking. "I was in complete turmoil," Leanne says. "I was trying to make it on my own and I was failing dismally. I felt as if all was lost."

In what Leanne calls an "ashes-to-phoenix" transition, a midlife crisis fostered such a profound change in her life that she rose to become owner and chief executive of a multimillion-dollar business that regularly earns coveted slots on best-company lists in her region.

You won't find Leanne's management rules in any Harvard Business School case study. Using leadership tactics forged in the crucible of midlife turbulence, Leanne mastered her external world by focusing within—by learning to go slower, to heed her intuition and instincts, to have fun and to embrace unexpected opportunities with confidence.

It is a paradox that arises over and over in the lives of women guided by the Leader, perhaps the most dramatic archetype: To transform your external world, work on inner needs.

From Sidelines to Center Stage. The Leader has long played roles scripted by others, then emerges at midlife with an overarching vision of her own. This archetype is all about making one's distinct and inventive mark on the world, in business, in politics, in philanthropy, or in the community. In my study, some women in the Leader role formed businesses or rose to the helm of nonprofit organizations. Others blazed new trails in corporate management or ran for public office.

The Leader draws power from the basic human drive to take initiative. As laid out by pioneering personality theorist Erik Erikson, taking initiative involves mounting a positive response to the world's challenges, learning new skills, and feeling purposeful. Erikson held that mastering this skill, like the seven other psychosocial tasks he named, is essential to optimal personality development. Realizing one's vision and ideas, whether in a career, a business, a political campaign, or a nonprofit venture, is a way to take initiative, and also to lay the foundation for healthy aging.[1]

The realization that it is not too late at midlife to carve out such a direction-setting role can be tremendously energizing. This pattern has emerged in several long-term studies. Women show sharp increases between early adulthood and their mid-fifties in self-confidence, personal identity, responsibility, and risk-taking ability.[2] Professional women exhibit the same midlife increases in leadership potential and quality of judgment at midlife as professional men; they also become more serious, and less concerned with what others think of them.[3]

The female-owned businesses that are emerging as such a powerful economic force are dominated by women at this stage of life. A disproportionately high number of these companies are headed by women ages 35 to 54, Census Bureau data show—49 percent, compared with the 34 percent of the total female population that is in this age group.

The average age of members of the Women Presidents' Organization, a New York–based organization with fifty chapters nationwide, is about 55. Many of these women, who run businesses with at least $1 million to $2 million in annual revenue, founded their companies in their late thirties or early forties because they were no longer willing to make the compromises required to work for someone else. They want "more control over their time and their compensation, and more influence," says Marsha Firestone, WPO founder and president.

Heidi, a Boston marketing specialist in my study, rocketed through the ranks at the high-tech company where she worked for a decade. But a series of restructurings and management changes of the kind that have come to characterize corporate life left her so stressed and frustrated that she was nearly disabled by chronic neck pain. Unable to move her head, she saw a series of doctors and chiropractors. None were able to heal her.

Finally, at age 50, she quit to found her own business. Within weeks, the pain was gone. Her company has grown to ten employees and evolved into a family business that employs her adult daughter.

Organizations that advise them see women in their forties and fifties leaving corporations in large numbers. Hedy Ratner, who as co-president of the Women's Business Development Center, Chicago, counsels growing numbers of midlife women, describes these enterprising women as educated, smart, experienced, and creative. They ply all those skills, she says, to escape oppressive job environments and spread their wings.[4]

Harvard Business School's Myra Hart, a cofounder of the office-supply chain Staples and an authority on female entrepreneurs, says these women relish taking charge at midlife. They have seen aspects of business or life that need fixing, and they go to great lengths to set up situations where they not only can create but can control implementation of the solutions, products, processes, and culture.[5]

And they are changing the face of the economy. Women-owned companies employ 19.1 million people, produce $2.5 trillion in sales, and create jobs at roughly twice the overall rate for U.S. business, says the Center for Women's Business Research, a Washington, D.C., advocacy group.

Geraldine Laybourne, the talented cable-TV executive who

made the Nickelodeon network a powerhouse in children's programming, cites a midlife drive for leadership as a motivating factor in her decision to leave a top job at Disney/ABC Cable Television and, at age 51, to start Oxygen Media, an innovative network and the first completely owned and controlled by women. Her children were grown and, for the first time, she felt free to take a few financial risks.

At midlife, after taking risks for her employers for years, "now I need to take a risk for myself," Ms. Laybourne remembers thinking at the time. "This is the final stage of growing up. There's nobody to blame but me" for the outcome. "It all stops here."

This archetype will help mold the workplace of the next twenty years. Women in the 45- to 54-age range now make up 10.9 percent of the workforce, up from 7.5 percent in 1990. Among the 36 percent of these middle-aged women workers who might be expected to experience midlife crisis, a significant minority are likely to be motivated by the desire to exercise leadership. This trend is certain to raise executive-suite awareness of ageism and sexism and alter corporate policies and practices.

Latent Leadership. Leanne's early career was a story of false starts. The daughter of a roofer, she worked her way through undergraduate school in a remarkable variety of skilled jobs, from window-display management to teaching. She was planning to found a publishing venture after graduation. But the plan fell by the wayside when she met the man who would become her husband.

Uncertain of her goals, Leanne considered entering law school after she got married but doubted she had the brains to get in. She took a stab at it and surprised herself by making high scores on the LSATs, winning early admission to a prestigious program, and being named in her first year to a coveted clerkship. But she found she did not like the work and dropped out. She also started an M.B.A. she did not finish.

The pattern of false starts was reinforced by her husband's job in sales, which forced the family to relocate four times in sixteen years. Leanne, a slender, petite woman with shoulder-length brown hair, large eyes, and a youthful, heart-shaped face, began a part-time personal coaching business and taught self-improvement seminars. But all the moving, plus trying to be Supermom to their two sons, kept her from pursuing much of a career.

Leanne's midlife crisis exploded in classic Sonic Boom mode as she neared her forties. She had grown tired over the years of trying to achieve the emotional intimacy she wanted with her husband, who remained distant despite efforts to solve the problem in counseling. In the first of a series of bitter blows, Leanne's marriage fell apart. A few months later, her father died.

Then, her two restive teenage boys rebelled. Leanne asked for help from her ex-husband, who had quickly remarried. The boys moved in with him, and they soon relocated across the country. Devastated at the loss of her boys and facing severe financial problems, including foreclosure on her house, Leanne reached the breaking point. "I felt like everything was lost," she says.

In her despair, Leanne put the principles she had been teaching in her self-improvement seminars to a test. She made a decision: She would let go of the things she had lost and stop focusing on her neediness.

"It was a turning point when I decided to stop holding on to the misery—the lack, the fear, the scarcity, the bills I owe, the kids I don't have here with me. I decided, if I wind up in the street, it can't be as bad as living in this emotional torment." She made a conscious decision to begin focusing on what she had, rather than what she lacked.

She moved into a rental home and started working as a temp in lowly filing and clerical jobs. Her first paycheck was for $104, and her rent was $1,000. "I looked at it and forced myself to feel grateful for everything I had, and to stop looking at everything I didn't. It sounds simple, and it is. But it started a change in my world."

Good things started coming her way. A temp position in marketing at a big mortgage company brought a job offer and a series of speedy raises and promotions. Her boss quit to start his own company and asked her to be a senior executive. As her responsibilities grew, she strived to keep having fun rather than "getting caught up in the corporate stuff, getting caught up in my boss's frenetic energy, getting caught up in the deadlines," she says. "I'd constantly bring myself back to, 'Is this stress what you want to feel?' The answer was always no. I want to feel excited. I want to feel creative. I want to be grateful for all the things that are going right."

Next came a chance to run a marketing company with a silent partner. Leanne seized the opportunity and soon bought out her partner and grew the company to $3 million in revenue and thirty-five employees. Under Leanne's leadership, the firm has been named one of Colorado's "best places to work," listed among its leading privately held companies, and named one of 100 top woman-owned companies in her state.

Leanne runs her business on principles that would make the typical CEO blanch—tenets she learned in her own darkest hours. Goals make her anxious, so she refuses to set any. She believes work should be fun. "We're real productive, but fun is high on the priority list," she says. She gives employees team lunches and regularly brings in a masseuse. "We try to make work about the people, rather than the business." She adds, "It creates a synergy of a great environment, where people are appreciated and they do what they love. And it works."

Leanne sees her success springing from a distinctly feminine leadership style. She rejects what she considers "the masculine role model that is about willpower, about stomping on whatever you need to, to make your point." She also has left behind what she regards as a female custom of "martyring ourselves," she says. Instead, she has found a leadership philosophy that works for her: "Standing in your own power, with your will and your love at the same time, and being present in the moment."

Other realms of her life are richer, too. One of Leanne's sons has returned to Colorado to work for her; "it is a joy to see him on a regular basis," she says. She has had a series of increasingly better relationships with men, each bringing her closer to the kind of intimacy she wanted but failed to experience in her marriage.

And Leanne reaps growing satisfaction from a renewed spiritual life. She has replaced the agnosticism of early adulthood with belief in a higher power. "I've learned that if you learn to live your life as fully, authentically, and joyously as you can, you can't help but bring that light to other people. All you have to do is ask, and be willing to listen. And huge abundance will come."

Seeding the Future. Many Leaders are inspired to serve the broader community by entering politics. Some regard running for office as a way of building a better world for their children, of achieving the generativity that psychologists see as seminal to midlife development. Reflecting this desire, the average age of women in state legislatures is over 40.

The departure of two of Judy Goodman's three children for college left a gap she wondered at first how to fill. Goodman, who was not a part of my study, had a varied career as a counselor, broadcast journalist, and public relations consultant, as well as broad experience as a community volunteer. But at midlife, she wanted something more.

She accepted an invitation of a kind she had turned down in the past: to run for alderman of her small Missouri city. Goodman won the election and has found she loves her new role. Attending to concerns such as safety and economic development has been surprisingly fulfilling. She sees these decisions shaping quality of life for her friends, her neighbors, and her region.

At age 54, "I feel like I've been reborn as somebody who has a bigger vision," Goodman says. "I feel like I've gone to the next step, beyond me and my children to caring for the whole community." She loves pondering such questions as, "What do we value as a community? What will make our quality of life good for us and for our children, for the next generation?" This new role is so compelling, she says, that "I think about zoning and ordinances and codes in my sleep."

Answering higher callings does not come easy. It has forced Goodman to grow. During her campaign against a well-known, respected male opponent, Goodman had a natural tendency to talk with supporters about her anxieties and fears, using the people around her as a sounding board. In what she calls a "huge" step toward growth, she overcame that. "I realized that to be a leader, you have to lead. You need to inspire people and share the confidence you have in our own abilities," she says. She swallowed her fear and began emphasizing her vision and goals.

Coming face-to-face with fear is one hallmark of the Leader's transformation. As Cindy's story shows, loosening its paralyzing grip is a process that can take years.

Beyond Volunteering. Midlife crisis for Cindy exploded at age 40. She had dropped out of college to marry her high school sweetheart, then worked to support him as he earned his degree. Raised as a child to believe she was incapable of handling money or making financial decisions, Cindy placed her faith in her husband. For most of two decades she tried, as he wanted, to submerge herself in home and kids. A friend told her, "You're like the mom in [the film] *Pleasantville*," a prim, hovering 1950s woman in bows and sculpted curls, childlike and predictable on the surface, but simmering with unexpressed passion and strength beneath.

Cindy's marriage did provide a backdrop for a seemingly pleasant life, with lots of socializing and travel. But defining herself as a housewife/helpmate "was completely a role. It was never me," Cindy says. Restless, she plunged into one volunteer job after another, scattering her energies. Her husband began to do the same. But instead of constructive pursuits, he went out drinking with friends.

The irony of Cindy's weak self-image—her belief that she was incapable of managing money—was glaringly obvious to everyone but her. In her community work, she always kept the organizations she ran on budget. Gradually, she took more control at home. When her husband neglected their household finances, she hired a financial planner. She also finished college and opened a successful retail store with a partner.

Her fortieth birthday party marked a turning point. "I looked over at my husband, who was drinking a lot at that time. He just embarrassed me so. I remember thinking, 'Who *is* that person?'" Shortly after that, the sudden death of her mother, a "best friend" who had helped Cindy with her children and supported her in every way, brought more sadness.

Cindy had shared much with her mother; both women were enterprising and energetic but, at their husbands' behest, had curbed their drive to stay home. Cindy's mother stayed that course for her entire life. "She just stuck it out," Cindy says. In her grief and disillusionment, it struck Cindy that her mother's life had been largely wasted. Also, the responsibility for caring for Cindy's aged father shifted at that point to Cindy, a burden her husband resented. After a year of marriage counseling, they divorced.

In the months that followed, Cindy's life unraveled beyond recognition. Embarrassed to be the only single person among her married friends, she stopped going out. "My whole social life came to a dead halt," she says. "It threw me into a total tailspin. I had no idea who I was any longer. I was in a complete daze. I felt pathetic." She adds, "The thing that frightened me most was the lack of security. I wondered, 'How will I live?'"

Only after her worried children started coming home from college just to "hang out" with her did Cindy force herself to act. She enrolled in school again to study management—with no particular goal in mind except taking care of herself.

In time, she began realizing that the years she had spent in volunteer work were valuable. Cindy organized a successful campaign to create a full-time paying post for a parks director in her town, then applied for the job and won it through a competitive selection process. "It was a unique opportunity to put my own imprint" on the community, Cindy says. Her efforts have resulted in several new projects, beautified the city, and won praise from merchants' and real estate groups.

"I believe people's environments have a big impact on how they feel, and on how they maneuver through their day," she says. Providing a supportive milieu for others "really does lend purpose to life."

On the home front, Cindy has learned how to make investments and select insurance. She fulfilled a personal dream by buying investment property and is considering buying more. "I'm forcing myself," she says. "It's very scary, but I'm doing okay."

She feels she has taken charge of her relationships, too. Through a dating service, she met and fell in love with a man her age, a scientist. At first she insisted on preserving her single lifestyle during the week, confining romance to the weekends. Then, as they contemplated the next step, she told him, "I really want to live with you, but I don't want to be a 'wife'—to come home and make dinner and clean the house." Cindy's fiancé relishes her independence.

Although Cindy still feels fearful sometimes, taking leadership in her community and her financial affairs has helped her develop a more mature attitude toward risk. With the wisdom of her 50 years, she now understands that everything in life is impermanent. She held on to an antique dining-room set for years, for example, thinking of it as "the set I would have until I was eighty, the set I'd use when my grandkids came over for Thanksgiving turkey," she says. Recently, she placed it in storage to make way for her fiancé's more modern furniture.

"It has taken me a long time to realize that nothing is forever—nothing," Cindy says. "I'm trying to look at things with a lighter eye."

High Stakes. Much is at stake for individual women who have repressed their leadership drive. Research shows women who relegate themselves to the background in their twenties and thirties, by choosing jobs that underuse their talents or by denying themselves a desired career or community role, often have midlife regrets. A study of 3,000 middle-aged women, controlled for the effects of social background, resources, and physical health, found that those who were not fulfilling their career aspirations by midlife were significantly more depressed and felt less of a sense of purpose.[6]

The women in my study who were drawn into Leader roles have made major contributions as a result of their crises. At 48, one founded a consulting company in the Midwest that changed the thinking of thousands of managers and executives on the management issues she handles.

A San Francisco woman, neck-deep in midlife crisis at age 48, took a new job as a manager of a customer-service department and developed novel techniques to protect her agents from abuse by customers, to allow them to vent frustration, and to enable them to laugh about stress. Thanks to her newfound leadership skills, employee turnover in the department plunged and the quality of service soared.

Clearly, as the Leader emerges in women in the coming years, their impact in the marketplace, and on society as a whole, will deepen.

6

✦ ✦ ✦

THE ARTIST

We are here to abet creation and to witness it, to
notice each other's beautiful face and complex nature
so that creation need not play to an empty house.

—ANNIE DILLARD

At 50, it seemed Ruth was cruising the high road of life—enjoying good health, a prestigious editing career, marriage to a wonderful man, a thriving teenage son. It was only after darkness fell each evening, after she drifted off to sleep, that Ruth had trouble holding it all together.

Between midnight and dawn, dramatic characters emerged in Ruth's semiconsciousness, having dialogues and acting out dramas. The people and plotlines so energized her that she would rise from bed to sit at her computer for hours and capture them on paper. "These ideas would start to haunt me, and I would have to get up and write them down," she says. "It was almost as if these characters were living inside of me. They would start speaking and I would go to my computer and write what they were saying."

She had never written a play in her life. Yet now, night after night, week after week, she was haunted by dramas of the mind. Her characters' dialogues grew into relationships, the relationships grew into plotlines, and the plotlines grew into pages and pages of drafts of full-blown plays. Ruth soon had seventeen file folders filled with plays or dialogues. She began dreaming of becoming a playwright, of having a play produced on Broadway.

"The dream wouldn't leave me alone," Ruth says. Her characters began hijacking her waking hours, too. "Driving to work and coming home, I'd be in this reverie. How can I do this play, and that play? That's all I was thinking about."

Ruth's dream would soon overtake her life, changing her career, her social and financial status, and her outlook on life. It was as if she had no choice. Finding her voice as a playwright "was an awakening of a part of my soul, an awakening to my true essence, to something deep inside of me that needed to be expressed," she says. "I think if I had ignored it it would have made me very sick."

A Core Calling. The Artist is a deeply passionate archetype that tends to turn women's values upside down at midlife, reorganizing their entire lives around one core calling: creating their art. Among Artists in my study, most described the experience as being swept away by a current so strong that it transformed not only them, but their relationships with spouses, children, and friends.

These women had usually been sidetracked in their twenties and thirties in a way that stifled the artistic dreams of their youth. They were drawn to a different path by child-rearing, breadwinning, or the imperatives of achieving success in business. Then, after decades of drowning out the voice of self-expression, their creative side exploded at midlife.

Researchers have documented a pattern of emerging creativity at midlife. In a study of a community of folk artists ranging in age from the thirties to early fifties, one researcher found a strong link between creativity and advancing age. The older artists were the most creative. Their thinking and planning processes were freer than younger artists', and they were less egotistical and more relaxed and open to new ideas.[1]

The importance of art to a woman's happiness in the last half of life can hardly be overestimated. In a landmark fifty-year study of adult development, Harvard professor and psychiatrist George Vaillant found that building creativity into one's life in middle age, along with learning to play and gaining younger friends, add more to one's enjoyment of life than does a high retirement income.[2]

The Artist also serves an important psychological purpose at midlife: It enables us to sublimate our pain into creativity. Sublimation is the psychological tool that directs a primitive or low human impulse into one that is ethically or culturally higher. It elevates our basal human instincts into purity or excellence, by transforming or refining them. Sublimation is among the highest human capabilities.

As losses and emergent instinctual drives threaten to overwhelm us at midlife, the Artist enables us to sublimate them. It revives a sense of wonder and helps us work through and resolve inner conflicts.

Midlife adults dwell in life's prime time for creativity. By this age, adults have accumulated a lot of practical know-how, as well as what psychologists call "crystallized" intelligence—accumulated specific information, such as knowing synonyms for an unusual word. But many middle-aged adults are not yet experiencing another change in the brain associated with old age—a decline in "fluid" intelligence, or the creative and flexible thinking needed to deal with novelty. Thus midlife is in some ways the optimal time for making new creative and intellectual contributions.[3]

Recent discoveries in cognitive neuroscience suggest that creative activities undertaken in midlife crisis may actually stimulate the middle-aged brain to grow and develop new capabilities. Experiments show the brain has a remarkable capacity to respond to new challenges. The Artist, and in fact all the archetypes in this book, may actually stimulate the brain to sprout additional dendrites—extensions that make connections with other cells—and to develop new synapses, the contact points between cells. As a woman stays engaged with vital, stimulating activities these changes continue despite the aging process.[4]

The psychological drive to create may peak at this stage, too. Pioneering psychoanalyst Carl Jung and Elliot Jacques, the man who coined the term *midlife crisis*, both stressed the importance of coming to terms with one's creative potential as a central task at midlife.[5]

The Artist archetype bears risks; a life of poverty is not the least among them. But the rewards are many: self-expression beyond measure, the joy of affirmation when others see and appreciate your message to the world, and a firmer sense of personal identity.

This archetype also bears rich meaning beyond oneself: the gift of being able to "transport" others to a higher level of experience. Countless communities are enriched by the Artist, as middle-aged women turn their energies to making art, creating and performing in theatrical productions, or otherwise contributing to the cultural and artistic life of all those they touch.

Nighttime Awakenings. For as long as she could remember, Ruth loved to perform, and to uplift others by performing. Her parents enjoyed theatre and music, and Ruth sang and danced for them as a child. "My mother thought I would be the next Shirley Temple. She very much encouraged me," Ruth recalls. She dreamed of becoming an actress.

But Ruth's dream derailed when she was 11. Her mother died, and "I lost my greatest support," Ruth says. She was sent to boarding schools while her father traveled for his work. Her dancing and acting lessons fell by the wayside. "I left behind my absolute passion," she says.

Traces of the dream stubbornly surfaced from time to time. Vocational-preference testing in her twenties showed Ruth had an overwhelming aptitude for the theatre, scoring ten points higher than her second-strongest field, journalism. But the counselor who administered the test steered Ruth away from theatre. For the next twenty-five years Ruth took more practical jobs, as a legal secretary, then as a writer and editor.

Not surprisingly, she met the man she would marry while pursuing a performance art—folk dancing. They married in the United States, then moved to Ontario.

Grieving for her mother was a constant motif in Ruth's life. She seriously considered attending medical school, a leaning she attributes to "a bit of hypochondria because my mother died so young." She says that after an evening spent watching a film about a mother-daughter relationship, *The Divine Secrets of the Ya-Ya Sisterhood*, "I cried my eyes out." The movie evoked so many memories of her mother who, like many adult women in the 1950s, worked outside the home only briefly.

"She got a job as a secretary and she was miserable. She tried it for three months and all she did was type all day. She got a five-minute tea break and a half-hour lunch break and another five-minute tea break. Then she had to come home and take care of us," Ruth recalls.

As Ruth's midlife crisis gained momentum, remembrances of her mother assumed a consuming importance. She dreamed one night of having a long conversation with her. "I sat down at the computer and wrote for three hours straight," Ruth says. In the conversation the two women compare their perspectives on work and family, and the tenor of their very different lives. "I would have given my eyeteeth to have a career," the mother tells her daughter. The daughter replies that she would love to stay home with her kids, but instead feels she has to do both—work and care for the children.

Inspired by her dream of a life in the theatre, Ruth helped organize a playwriting program at a women-run playhouse in her city, and helped start a playwriting program there. She performed in community musical-theatre productions, and hired a playwriting coach to help her polish her scripts.

Seeing Ruth's life transformed, her teenage son asked her one day why she had gone into journalism. The question recalled a memory she had forgotten—of the vocational test she had taken nearly twenty-five years earlier. She dug it out of an old file and was startled to see just how strongly the test had signaled her theatrical talents—and how deeply she had buried that sign. "I felt vindicated," Ruth says. "I knew I was on the right path."

Although Ruth's creative energies were increasingly crowding out other thoughts, she feared quitting her high-paying editing job. She was afraid of losing the income. But her husband supported her desires, and on long walks together they laid plans that eventually gave Ruth the courage to quit.

"When I finally made that decision to leave, then things just completely calmed down. My fears went away," Ruth says. Her income has plummeted and the transition has not been easy. "It's a hard thing, but it's a good thing. I'm happier now than I have been in years."

For Ruth, giving voice to the Artist was more than a means of self-expression. It was a way to connect with the memory of the beloved mother she had lost. Amid her midlife turmoil, Ruth learned at last to give herself the same kind of encouragement she had received decades earlier, in such abundance, from her mother.

The Artist role also affords Ruth a means of connecting with other people in a deep and meaningful way. Asked to explain the meaning of her art, Ruth recalls a moment after a production in which she had played a singing and acting role. A stage manager, a woman in her thirties, approached her.

"I really love watching you on stage," the woman said. Ruth thanked her, and the woman added gratefully, "You just transport me."

Tears sprang to Ruth's eyes. "I was so touched. Theatre is about transporting people. It is about taking people out of their day-to-day world and creating some magic, giving them some relief from the mundane." In that, she adds, "I feel like I connect with the universe. I believe that what we do through the arts becomes spiritual. It takes us to another realm. And I feel really good when I do it."

Stilling the Inner Censor. For many women, creating art at midlife engages not only the soul but the body. Ruth is convinced that the hormonal changes caused by menopause helped spark the explosion of creativity in her life. Researchers who have examined the female brain before and after menopause have not found any measurable differences in functioning. However, many women do find menopause sufficiently jarring that it prompts them to undertake new activities.

One researcher, Mona Lisa Schulz, a physician and author of *The New Feminine Brain*, believes that the same hormonal changes that cause moodiness, irritability, and impulsivity associated with menopause also cause "emotionally creative circuits [to] become unbridled." As a result, "a woman is less likely to judge and censor her creative drives."[6]

For Helena, the emergence of the Artist engaged her body *first:* She took up an old childhood dream of becoming a figure skater, reveling in the physical beauty of the sport's speed and iceborne flight. Then slowly, through a painstaking painting project that consumed her creative energies for nearly three years, Helena reengaged her body in the visual arts that had been her core focus in her twenties and early thirties—"teaching" her hands to know again the brushes, the strokes, and the images of her art, as they had known them decades earlier, before work, marriage, and children eclipsed Helena's budding artistic career. Her story shows how powerfully the Artist supersedes and reorders all other values in a woman's life around a core driving passion to create.

An Explosive Experience. A casual observer might have thought Helena had it made. At 47, she was co-proprietor with her husband of a bustling Hudson Valley restaurant and B&B. Working as maître d' each weekend evening, she helped entertain crowds of fashionable guests. Some drove more than a hundred miles just to dine at their establishment.

But inside Helena was dying. Once a respected artist with a

growing reputation in Manhattan, she had given up her career thirteen years earlier to be a wife, a working mother, and a business partner with her husband. Although she tried several times to set up studio space in various rooms in the hotel, "I didn't have enough quiet and the kids were there and the waiters were running up and down the stairs and cleaning people were doing laundry," she says. "And I couldn't make art."

Her marriage, too, had wilted under the strains of business, child-rearing, and neglect. Bustling about to serve her guests, Helena says, "I felt like an old peacock with my tail dragging behind me."

It was in the physical realm that Helena began the hard work of midlife crisis. She started insisting on leaving the B&B daily to work out at a gym. "I felt like I was getting fat and ugly and I didn't want my life to end like that," she says. As she restored her connection with her body, her old dream of figure skating gained power. Helena had trained as a child with a noted figure-skating coach. "My greatest dreams of freedom always involved me skating with great abandon," she says.

In what she describes as "an explosive experience," she decided one day to start skating again. "Okay, I've had it," she thought. "I'm finally going to do something for myself." She and her daughter, then seven, began trekking twice weekly to an ice rink an hour's drive away, to study with two well-regarded coaches. "I'd take a lesson and she'd take a lesson. It was very powerful for both of us," Helena recalls.

She sighs with delight as she remembers how it felt to fly over ice again. "One of the great regrets of my life is that I waited so long. Jumping! It was fabulous! Skating backward as fast as you can, turning and leaping into the air. . . . It was wonderful!"

"Why don't you try a sit spin?" the coach asked her one day.

Helena hesitated, struggling to recall how to do the difficult maneuver, then tried it and settled into it instantly. "My body still knew how to do it, from when I was a girl," she says. "It was like physical archaeology," unearthing muscular knowledge buried by years of disuse. The self-deception characteristic of midlife crisis soon caught up with Helena, however. She ignored mounting pain in her knees, pretending she was fine until the knee damage forced her to stop skating altogether and have surgery.

Although Helena's knees were never the same, "I wouldn't give up that attempt to skate for the world," she says.

Escape to the Rose Room. The part of Helena that inspired her to start skating again, what she calls the "expressive part of myself," began demanding more attention.

Helena had been an intermedia artist of some repute in the 1980s. She had a master's degree from a top art school, conducted workshops and presentations, and received two prestigious federal arts grants. But the years of child-rearing and hard work at the B&B had severed Helena's inner connection with her art. She became so estranged from her own creativity that she could not bear to look at paintings when she visited the city.

Although she had no time to spare, Helena began stealing away from the B&B to work on a decorative painting project in a friend's lakeside home. There, a spacious room, with blank walls and French doors opening toward the dawn, awaited what her friend Ann, the home's owner, envisioned as a room-sized mural. In what would become a watershed project, Helena worked for most of the next three years to transform the room with a sweeping display of dozens of giant, deeply colorful painted roses in various stages of bloom. In the slow work on what came to be known as the Rose Room, Helena reconnected with her talent. She embraced "the absolute philosophy that I was going to let anything happen," she says. "It was a way to enter back into my work as an artist."

Laboring hour by hour in the womblike silence of the room, Helena's hands remembered how to paint. She scattered blossoms fully twenty inches in breadth or more, pink, lavender, yellow, red, across the walls, their green leaves shaded with traces of silver. Floating as if airborne, some were mere buds, some widened in full bloom, and others waned against the pale-yellow walls in what seemed to Ann a metaphor for entering life's last half. Along the edges of the pale blue-to-lavender ceiling, sponged into a soothing pattern, Helena painted freehand the lines of a Seamus Heaney poem of renewal and hope, "The Sea Change."

Today, everyone who sees the Rose Room loves it, Ann says. It has become "a place of great happiness." Sometimes, Ann falls asleep reading in the room and dreams of her grandmother's rose garden, of walking there with her grandmother long ago.

The Rose Room touched off a creative renaissance for Helena. "I decided I was going to live out my life as an artist, no matter what I had to do to do it." She began spending a significant amount of her time making art, working with a new collage form that combines oil paint, sculpture, and digital prints. "I feel like I'm a twenty-year-old defining my life," Helena says. "And I'm not done yet. I'm doing all the things I probably should have been doing in my thirties."

Meanwhile, the stresses and overwork of running the B&B had undermined Helena's marriage beyond repair. She and her husband divorced and sold the business, and Helena sank to an emotional low. At 47, she moved into a tiny apartment with two pre-teenage daughters, not much cash, and little space or time for herself. She took two part-time jobs teaching art. In rare moments alone, in her car running errands or driving to pick up her kids, she sometimes would begin crying, "in total fear at what was going to happen to me," she says. "I was dying a spiritual death that took me so low, it felt like a physical death."

With support from friends, she began to make a new life with room at the center for art. Helena managed to buy a dilapidated, historic old house and renovate it with friends' help. "I've had to be very inventive to survive," she says. She lives near her ex-husband and the two are successfully co-parenting their daughters.

Losing her way, then finding it again, has taught Helena a new perspective. "I'm so careful now what I do in my life. I know now that if you make one incorrect step down the wrong path, that path defines you and sometimes it's not easy to get off it." Now, she is letting the Artist guide her toward a path uniquely her own. "I'm out there with my machete, chopping down palms and trying to make space for myself to grow."

There are moments of doubt. On days when her back aches

from all the driving she does between her jobs and her home, she questions her decisions. She worries about money. "It would be so easy to get a job as a manager or an administrator. But I'd be back in the same place," doing work she hates.

For now, at least, the answer is clear: "The intellectual freedom to design my life and my art is more important to me than anything, at this point." She pauses, then adds, "Where it's driving me, I don't know. But I'm an optimist."

7

• ✦ •

THE GARDENER

You must live in the present, launch yourself on every wave, find your eternity in each moment.

— HENRY DAVID THOREAU

By her early fifties, Melanie's midlife crisis had taken her about as low as a woman can go. She had lost her father to cancer, then shouldered the burden of caring for three aged relatives. She suffered a disabling inner-ear injury and lost her sexual vitality to a hysterectomy. Then Melanie's only child announced he was gay.

Melanie plunged into a suicidal despair. "I felt powerless for the first time in my life. I simply felt old and completely 'over,'" she says. "I could not be by myself. Any time I was by myself, I was in tears—the shower, wherever."

Melanie resisted the impulse to end her life and, four years later, has managed to begin feeling good again. The archetype of her midlife crisis offers no adrenaline rush, no public plaudits or recognition. It's a path barely anyone notices. Yet it is sensuous, beautiful, absorbing, and abundant.

Melanie immersed herself in making the most of the world around her—developing worthwhile hobbies, creating splendor in her own realm, and finding joy in small things. She designed a garden rich in symbols of her family history. She found ways of creating beauty, experimenting with photography and gift cards. And she undertook community service, teaching English to refugees and visiting hospice patients.

A Restrained Archetype. Candide, the hero in Voltaire's classic eighteenth-century novel by that name, has become a cultural symbol of the philosophy Melanie practices. Candide travels the world, discovers much evil, and comes to a time of discouragement and disillusionment. At midlife, he concludes that the best path to wisdom lies in tending his own garden—in investing his work, care, and attention upon that part of the world he can control, the only part, he has come to believe, that holds any promise of fulfillment and peace.

The garden is useful as both a model and a metaphor in the later stages of life, says Harvard University's George Vaillant. Good gardeners are by definition generative, he points out. They produce flowers, fruits, and fragrances to enjoy. They create beautiful places on the earth that endure beyond one season. When they die, their gardens live on after them, instilling a kind of immortality. The garden can also be a lesson in humility; people can do their work, but then they must let go and let Nature take its course.

The Gardener is a temperate archetype, one that motivates a woman to live in the moment and to savor all that her senses can absorb from the world around her. Instead of ripping her life apart to pursue some new prize, adventure, or endeavor, the Gardener focuses inward and on her immediate surroundings. She ventures onto relatively traditional midlife paths, investing in existing relationships, hobbies, voluntarism, neighborhood service, or home projects.

The Gardener derives power from a psychological need for creativity and generativity. She sublimates the pain and impulses of midlife crisis into a higher cultural or ethical good. Sewing, gardening, pottery throwing, and flower arranging all served as creative play for women in the Harvard Study of Adult Development.[1]

Despite the restraint of this archetype, it is anything but austere. The Gardener's impact can be sensuous and energizing. To the extent that it brings a woman fully alive—fully attuned to her own senses and soul, and drinking in the joys they can bring—the Gardener can be as engaging and colorful as the Lover. The Gardener can alter women's lives as profoundly as any other archetype. Just as a traveler who changes course by one degree at the beginning of a long journey can end up on a different continent, a woman who makes Gardener-type adjustments in her life can wind up with an entirely different life years hence.

Signs of the Gardener abound in our culture. Gardeners place a high value on community, as do midlife women in general. More than 78 percent of women ages 45 to 59 rate being a productive member of one's community and society as extremely important, compared with only 70 percent of men, an AARP study shows.[2]

These values lead middle-aged women to volunteer at a significantly higher rate than other demographic groups. Some 36 to 40 percent of women ages 35 to 54 give their time to worthy causes. That is several percentage points higher than the 29 percent of men in the same age group and than any other age or gender group in the population as a whole, U.S. Labor Department data show. Four-fifths of women age 50 and over cite helping others as a core personal goal, a study by the Simmons School of Management reports. That, too, is several percentage points higher than women in any other age group, including girls in the typically idealistic stage of adolescence. Three-fourths of 50-and-over women also say contributing to their communities is of central importance in their lives.[3] In another sign, midlife women are more satisfied with the quality of their contribution to others than men. Social responsibility also rises to new highs among women in middle age, a pattern that does not emerge among men.[4]

The Gardener bears risks and rewards. This archetype tends to do less harm to social supports, such as employment and relationships. In that, it can set the stage for a rich and stable old age. However, this restrained archetype may not be fully satisfying for some women. It may fall short of fostering the personal growth they desire.

Crosscurrents of Love. Melanie's childhood was idyllic by some measures, repressive by others. As the daughter of a World War II hero and a stay-at-home mom in the 1950s, she enjoyed great freedom growing up. "I could get on a bicycle and ride for miles and be not only totally safe, but be flying along, having my wonderful little ten-year-old life riding around the countryside, whenever I wanted," she recalls.

Her mother was so nurturing that when Melanie skinned her knee, she would paint a face on it with iodine and fix chicken soup to make Melanie feel better. She was also very close to her father, a tall, athletic man; he taught her to bowl and ride a bike. Her mother told stories of her father's heroism as a bombardier, how he curled his six-foot frame into the nose of a B-52 and dropped bombs over Germany in the war.

As loving as her parents were, other influences held Melanie back. Although a part of her yearned to see the world, family life was bounded by her father's postwar wish to be "devoted to normalcy," to live in their Pennsylvania city and, after the devastation he had seen, to "never go anywhere again," Melanie says.

The sexism of that era seeped into Melanie's upbringing. She received less encouragement than her brothers to go to college, and the career advice she heard from adults was typical of that generation: Become a teacher. "There were not a whole lot of female role models," she says. On the advice of teachers and school counselors, she did graduate from college, moved to Washington, D.C., and landed a series of staff jobs on Capitol Hill.

Her father's influence and example of bravery had shaped her consciousness, however, and Melanie charted a courageous course early in her career. When she discovered corruption in one congressman's back-office operations, she became outraged and took the story to a newspaper. "I was so full of righteous indignation," she says. The story ran and Melanie was summarily fired.

Working on staff for a lobbying organization in a subsequent job, she bucked bosses' expectations that she wash the coffee cups, as was expected of all women in that office. Her suggestion to substitute disposable cups drew fire at high levels—"It's not up to you to make suggestions to us," her boss huffed—and she got the ax again.

Melanie soon began making career decisions she would later regret. She passed up a ground-floor opportunity in public broad-casting, a field that later underwent explosive growth. She married, then quit her journalism career after she and her husband encountered fertility problems. She was too distracted to work full-time, she decided, and took up freelancing instead.

Looking back, Melanie wonders to what extent those decisions contributed to her midlife crisis. Although she and her husband were unable to conceive the numerous children they wanted, she did give birth to a son and Melanie focused largely upon raising him well. For most of her adult life, Melanie, a fit, vibrant woman with short dark hair and hazel eyes, regarded herself as a "happy, active, sensible person with a couple of good friends, a good marriage, and a lovable son."

Into the Void. It took decades for these crosscurrents to deepen into the whirlpool that threatened to suck Melanie under. The losses and setbacks of her late forties felt like death by a thousand cuts. Lacking the alternative focus of a career, Melanie felt more keenly the pain of her father's death, her growing elder-care duties, her hysterectomy, her son's coming-out. Menopause, a marker of the irrevocable end of her childbearing years, brought back her old regret over being unable to conceive more than one child.

Melanie was overcome by self-blame, shame, and regret. She jumped to the conclusion that because her son was gay, she had failed as a mother and the two became estranged. Harking back to the toughness of her bombardier father, Melanie dug in and searched her past for the cause of her troubles. She attacked herself for jumping off the career track years earlier. If only she had stayed in the working world, Melanie reasoned, her career would have provided an alternative focal point, a source of identity and comfort in a time of family strain. Instead, "I felt as though I had failed in every arena," she says.

Torn by inner conflict, she battled the urge to kill herself. Her pragmatic side told her she was experiencing a bout of depression. "But at the same time," Melanie recalls, "I also thought, 'I just don't think I can ever come out of this. I'd rather just go into the void. And be free.'"

Her husband, who regularly came home from work to find Melanie crying, was starting to feel overwhelmed. "You need to help yourself. You need to do whatever it is you need to do," he told her. "But just do it."

A Backyard Renewal. Melanie began edging back from the chasm. She started seeing a psychiatrist twice weekly. In those sessions, "I took baby steps back, back, back to that core of myself," she says—to the inner strengths that ultimately started her on a path to renewal. "The problem you're not focusing on," the psychiatrist told her, "is that you're in the middle of your life, and you need to find out what it is you want."

He helped her see that her son's sexuality was not the indictment she had made it out to be. Melanie began asking herself, "He's a good student, he's not on drugs. What is your problem?"

She realized she had been trying to live vicariously through her son. Without realizing it, "I was feeling that I had made lots of bad choices," she says. "I saw areas where I was just waiting for him to live out some of my unfulfilled goals." Instead, Melanie needed to get to work on herself, on "making my own legacy in other ways, without withdrawing my love from him."

Melanie lived out her midlife crisis in the Slow Burn mode. She plunged into gardening and created a rich universe in the backyard of her home's single acre of land. Starting with what had only a few years earlier been an empty lot, she planted flowers, shrubbery, blooming arbors, ground cover, and trees. She designed a three-season garden with plants that bloom in spring, summer, and fall.

Ducks, chipmunks, birds, and other creatures are drawn there, and lots of mating, hunting, and animal play go on. "Our backyard is a little bit like *Fantasia*," Melanie says. "The garden stimulates all the senses. That's what's so wonderful about it." She stresses plants with scents, such as lavender. "The leaves have a beautiful dusty color in the summertime, and that's a nice contrast to the dark foliage. And it gets a beautiful white blossom," she says. Sometimes she crushes the leaves and sprinkles them in her bedroom drawer. Lilies-of-the-valley ring the doorway, and clematis vines climb the arbor; Melanie twines the tendrils so the faces of the flowers turn toward her house.

Her garden evokes memories. Melanie sought out an old-fashioned flower, the hosta, and planted it as a remembrance of her grandmother. She remembers arriving as a child at her grandparents' rambling frame house for a visit; her grandmother always came running out from the kitchen to greet them next to a fragrant hosta bed. "She would always be there next to the hostas, ready to greet us with big hugs and lots of cheek pinching." Melanie found a variety with a fragrant flower and planted it right outside her kitchen window. The perfume drifts inside, over the kitchen table, whenever she opens the window.

The plantings remind her, too, of languorous summer days in her childhood, spent with her extended family on the front porch of her paternal grandparents' home. Adults and children clustered about a round wooden table, the men in ironed white shirts, the children in cotton sunsuits, quietly sharing puzzles and games as a tree-lined river flowed nearby.

"It was very relaxed," Melanie recalls. "Our grandfather taught us to play pinochle and gave us his paper rings from his cigars to wear. My grandmother would put big bowls of fruit out on the porch and several pitchers of lemonade. No one ever told you that you were going to spoil your dinner by eating or drinking too much. And you could spit your cherry pits over the porch railing, if the grown-ups weren't watching." The children vied for a coveted seat on the bench swing, which looked out on a river with geese and a field filled with wildflowers. Sometimes, Melanie rocked herself to sleep there.

The garden bears life lessons, too. As a small child, Melanie's son brought a tree seedling home from school one day. They planted it in the front yard but it kept getting run over by the lawnmower. Melanie decided to yank it out, then thought better of it: "It was like the tree was looking at me, saying, 'Take care of me.' It was just a little thing. So I took it to the back of the yard and staked it and I said, 'I've given you everything I can and now you're on your own.'"

The seedling was so far back in her yard that she forgot about it. Years later, in the midst of her midlife crisis, Melanie noticed the tree again. "This tree had not only survived, but it was now eight feet tall and it was beautiful," she says.

The tree, Melanie says, "was a metaphor for my son. You nurture something and it grows in ways that surprise you." As in life, "you don't have control. The garden symbolizes transition. It will grow according to the ways Nature wants it to—not necessarily in the way you want it to."

Enlisting the Arts. Intent on nurturing and interpreting the beauty around her, Melanie enrolled in art school and took up photography. "I found things in Nature, and I saw that if I just got very detailed and close to them, there was a whole other world, a world within a world," she says. "I felt I was pouring my heart out." She captured vivid shots of blossoms in her own garden, shooting into the sun and using paper as a reflector to produce Georgia O'Keeffe–type images. She experimented with special films and filters, creating unexpected colors and tones to lend an aged or "otherworldly" aura to her work.

On walks in the country, she turned her eye and her camera to "unusual scenes, like a farmer plowing his fields at sunset. That is pretty lyrical, if the sun is hitting it just right," Melanie says. She made note cards of some of her photos and gave them as gifts. In contrast with her elder-care experience, "I felt I was giving something of myself, but in a pleasurable way, not in an exhausting way." She had a few boxes printed up for sale in local gift shops, and they sold out within days.

Reaching Out. Community service also helped Melanie heal. She signed up her dog, a golden retriever, for training to serve as a therapy animal for hospice patients. Melanie has taught the dog tricks that make patients laugh. Her visits with the dying serve as a reminder to savor the moment. "When you're looking at someone who's about to take an uncharted journey, it's mystical in a sense. Even though their physical suffering is being alleviated by hospice care, they still know, this is it for their corporeal existence," she says. "It's always a reminder of the unexpected. You can be running down the street one moment and three months later be lying in a bed in hospice."

Melanie also gained perspective in volunteer work teaching English as a second language to adult immigrants. Tutoring refugees from the Middle East, from Eastern Europe, and other wartorn regions—"people who were really struggling with survival issues, whose lives had been in dramatic jeopardy"—she learned to appreciate what she has. One student was a refugee in her thirties who had been trained as a classical pianist at the Moscow Conservatory. In the United States the best job she could get was plucking chickens at a slaughtering plant.

"Here is this person who can sit down and play these beautiful classical pieces on the piano, using these same hands to pluck chickens," Melanie says. The woman's husband was an engineer who had been forced to take a laborer's job in construction. When she tried to find a better job, she was advised to clean people's houses. Her husband's pride was devastated, Melanie says. Melanie went shopping with the woman, helping her sort through lingerie departments to find underwear in the right sizes, and gave the couple symphony tickets as a gift.

Another student, a man in his fifties, had covered up his illiteracy all his adult life by relying on his wife to read for him. He came to Melanie for tutoring after his spouse died. "His cover was blown," Melanie says. She helped him get tested for learning disabilities, but the memory "stayed with me."

Her volunteer work "slapped me back a little bit into reality, into, 'Okay, things are bad but at least I'm not a refugee,'" like some of her students. "Their travails restored my perspective and reminded me how very lucky I am by sheer accident of birth."

Questioning Work-Family Choices. Research shows Melanie is not alone in questioning her past work-family decisions. More than half of the women in my study believed or at least suspected in midlife that they had applied the wrong formula for allocating their time and energies between work and family.

Cutting back on work to tend to child-rearing duties, as

Melanie did, takes a heavy psychological toll on women of her generation. While women who came of age in the 1940s and 1950s felt better about themselves after pulling back from the workplace for the sake of family, baby-boom women did not. In the MacArthur Foundation "Midlife in the United States" study, Melanie's contemporaries who compromised career for family scored significantly lower on questions about how well they liked themselves, how pleased they were with their lives and whether they felt satisfied with what they have accomplished.[5]

Melanie's failure to carve out a high-profile career remains a source of sadness. "That will always be a trouble spot for me," she says. Unlike some other women in my study, she believes she is too old to start a new career.

Nevertheless, her midlife crisis has brought her a measure of peace. She can count several rewards: "I find myself feeling good about things that are taking place, things that I do, interactions that I have. What else can you ask for?" In conversation these days, she laughs often. She keeps fit with weight training and plans to start new volunteer work at an elementary school, teaching students for whom English is a second language.

"I feel stronger that I got through it. I've proven to myself that I'm not going to lose my mind. I'm going to stay grounded," she says.

Melanie has found new ways to relate to her son, setting boundaries on conversation and pursuing simple pastimes, like playing Scrabble together. She has accepted that her son "is going to be who he is, not my fantasy of who he is going to be."

Melanie asked for assistance with her elder-care duties and got help from relatives with some of those time-consuming responsibilities. "I needed to stop trying to be all things to all people."

Like a fine metal alloy, her marriage was tested and proved strong enough to endure. She did not allow blame for her midlife crisis to spill over onto her husband, nor did she overburden the relationship. She gives her husband vast credit for his patience. "Maybe somebody else would have looked at me and said, 'You know, I cannot take you anymore and I am outta here.' But I believe he is in there for the long haul."

And they are still able to have fun together. After venturing onto the dance floor with her husband at a wedding, Melanie impulsively suggested they take swing dance lessons. He agreed, and they signed up together. "I think we're finally old enough," she says, "that we don't care who's laughing at us."

It is important to note that none of Melanie's painful circumstances changed. Instead, she changed her response to them, by degrees. "That's what happens in life. There are changes, and we either have to adapt to them," she says, "or we are crushed by them.

"When you're young you think, 'Well, I'll do this and everything will fall into place and I'll get an A.' But at age fifty-five you know that there's no way of going through life that's perfect," Melanie says. "And maybe that's the point, the perspective you're able to grasp in midlife."

8

$\cdot\ \blacklozenge\ \blacklozenge\ \blacklozenge\ \cdot$

THE SEEKER

Where does God dwell?
Wherever man lets Him in.

— HASIDIC PROVERB

As I began an interview with Aimee from Alabama, her first words answered a question I had not asked: "I need to tell you right up front—at no point in my midlife crisis did I do something really wonderful like move to Boulder and teach yoga. I have nothing like that to hold up and say, 'This is something for others to learn from.'"

The common midlife crisis stereotype sends people fleeing to a mountaintop, seeking out a guru, or joining a convent in a quest for spiritual meaning. Like most stereotypes, this one holds a kernel of truth. Aimee and many other women in my study hoped for spiritual fulfillment and regarded it as the best possible outcome of midlife turbulence. The Seeker is the archetype of this desire. It guides a woman's deep wish for connection with the religious, mystical, sacred, or truth-seeking side of herself.

The Seeker is the most complex and prevalent archetype in my study. Pursuit of spiritual fulfillment was primary for some. While not the dominant force for other women, the Seeker surfaced in a secondary role, acting as a foundation for growth, an inspiration to change, or a support in dark times.

Some Seekers in my study joined or became more active in established churches, synagogues, temples, or mosques. Others took nontraditional paths, following spiritual teachers who reach out via audiotapes, seminars, or the Internet. Still others took the private path of meditation, reading, and prayer, fostering their own relationship with a higher power or spiritual tradition.

The emergence of the Seeker in middle age is documented in the giant MacArthur Foundation study, "Midlife in the United States." Early spiritual and religious training has "a sleeper effect" on people's values and behavior that surfaces strongly at midlife, researcher Alice Rossi found. In early adulthood, people who grew up in families that placed high importance on religion and spiritual values show no greater concern for society and the welfare of the community than people who did not grow up in such families.

But by age 40 and above, people with religious backgrounds were significantly more likely than others to revive those values by showing greater concern for civic responsibility and contributing to the welfare of others. Thus in a classic midlife-crisis pattern, the Seeker, repressed in early adulthood, reemerges and ushers in a new life perspective at midlife.[1]

The Seeker shows up in culture and research in a variety of ways. Women over 40 are the most religious Americans, with religiosity taking a sharp leap upward in the 40- to 55-year-old bracket, according to recent findings from a Gallup poll. Midlife women are about 14 percentage points more likely than men in the same age group to describe religion as "very important" in their lives and to attend a church or synagogue "almost weekly or more."[2]

Middle-aged women also have been consistent in church attendance in the face of declines among men. While the proportion of middle-aged men who attend church often has declined by nine percentage points in the past decade to 38 percent, women ages 38 to 55 have held steady in church attendance.[3] About half of midlife women continue to attend church at least a dozen times a year, based on the long-term DDB Life Style Survey of 4,000 consumers.

The same pattern holds true for spirituality in general. Nearly 88 percent of women ages 45 to 59 say spirituality is extremely important to them, compared with less than 72 percent of men.[4] At religious seminars and churches of many stripes I have attended, midlife women far outnumber middle-aged men or people of any other age. Women, particularly women at midlife and beyond, tend to pray more often than men.[5]

The Seeker also shapes women's health. Spirituality is more closely linked to physical and psychological well-being in women than in men. Women in good physical and psychological health in a 1,465-person subset of the MacArthur Foundation

"Midlife" study reported that religion had far greater importance in their lives, compared with women in poor health. This pattern was less pronounced among men. Subjects' religious involvement was measured by the importance of religion in childhood, and by their reliance on spiritual beliefs for comfort and guidance. Psychological health was measured by questions gauging self-reliance, personal growth, and purpose in life, among other traits.[6]

Consciously or unconsciously, women no doubt sense the power of religion and spirituality in fostering good physical and emotional health. There is growing scientific evidence that the strength of this link has been underestimated. Gerontologists increasingly are studying religion's role in healthy aging. Conferences and books on gerontology now include rigorous studies and seminars on the link between a religious outlook and good health. Frequent church or synagogue attendance and self-reports of religiousness have been linked to higher self-esteem, happiness, and satisfaction, according to Jeff Levin, a Valley Falls, Kansas, scientist and author, and a pioneer in the emerging field of religious gerontology.[7]

Many women in my study, including Molly, whose story is told in this chapter, told of experiencing varieties of nontraditional spirituality. Levin found a significant increase between 1973 and 1988 in such phenomena, including déjà vu, a feeling that you have been somewhere before even though it is impossible, and spiritualism, or contact with the dead. Not only are these experiences more common among Americans than they were in the past, but they are increasing in successively younger age groups.[8] Levin sees potential "shifts toward a new spiritual consciousness" that do not necessarily surface in polls and surveys.[9]

Several women in my study drew support from religious traditions rooted in other cultures, such as Buddhism. Based on a thirty-year study by the National Opinion Research Center, those reporting a religion other than Protestantism, Catholicism, or Judaism reached nearly 7 percent of respondents, the highest level since the Center began the study in 1972.[10]

A Versatile Archetype. The Seeker plays a variety of roles in midlife crisis. Sometimes, it serves as a foundation for growth. Leanne, whose story of building one of Colorado's top businesses is told in chapter 5, spent much of her thirties seeking out a religious teacher and nurturing her spirituality. Her faith in turn gave her the courage to lift herself out of the slough of early midlife crisis and start her business. Like Leanne, many women in my study turned to spirituality for emotional support or guidance in decision making.

For others, the Seeker emerges as a missing piece. Some women who did not report some spiritual dimension to their midlife crises said they yearned for it. Emma from California, the sales representative profiled in chapter 4, never found sanctuary in spiritual pursuits, even though she was painfully anxious about her own mortality. "I'm not religious. I wish I were. People seem to get such comfort out of that, and I'm jealous," she said.

My findings affirm work by pioneering psychotherapist Carl Jung. Emphasizing that "religion" as he defined it had nothing to do with a particular creed or membership in an established church, Jung wrote that midlife healing is nearly always a process of finding spiritual or religious wholeness. Among all the hundreds of patients he had treated in the second half of life, Jung wrote, "there has not been one whose problem in the last resort was not that of finding a religious outlook on life. It is safe to say that every one of them fell ill because he had lost that which the living religions of every age have given to their followers, and none of them has been really healed who did not regain his religious outlook."[11]

Among all the women in my study, few had a more profoundly religious experience than Clare. In her newfound role of Seeker, she was able to reconnect with her best and deepest human qualities.

The Seeker as Guide. For Clare, crossing the threshhold of her county's big public hospital felt like a journey of a thousand miles. To serve as a volunteer lay chaplain to the hospital's neediest and most despairing patients, Clare had to leave behind the woman she had been for nearly a decade—the cofounder and hard-driving chief marketing executive of a fast-growing financial services start-up. Beset at age 50 by a midlife crisis, worried about her shaky health, and despairing over the dead-end course her life seemed to have taken, Clare felt cut off from herself and everything that had meaning to her.

Clare had grown accustomed to working with the heavy hitters of business, polished and skillful individuals who entered nearly every human encounter with an agenda. Seeking deeper meaning, she had signed on for a volunteer, multi-faith chaplaincy program, which trained her to approach people of all races, circumstances, and conditions in an accepting and peaceful way.

But to help the people she would see this day—the dying AIDS patient whose family had disowned her, the alcoholic bedeviled by delirium tremens, the drug addict whose inner voices drove him near suicide—truly to reflect "the loving presence of God," as she had been trained to do, Clare had to get down, way down, to a level of humility and vulnerability that had eluded her. She found herself fighting an urge to flee, a fear that she would prove unworthy of helping others.

Entering the general medical ward, she began a ritual to clear her mind and focus within. She plunged her hands and arms into a scrub basin and lathered up with lavish amounts of soap. Rubbing her skin, stripping off the bubbles, immersing her hands again in the water's warmth, Clare imagined her burdens dissolving and washing down the drain.

She took a deep breath. Trust the ritual, she told herself. Let the water do its work.

Starting down the hall, she plied another discipline she had developed for herself. Instead of yielding to instinct—approaching only certain patients who looked like her or her friends, or who were attractive, or who smelled okay or looked sane—she imagined herself as "the channel through which God's love for the patient will shine." She forced herself to check every room as she walked the corridor, knocking on every door where there was a patient who was awake. Carrying nothing in her hands, she entered each room, greeted each patient by name, and said simply:

"My name is Clare, I'm a chaplain in the unit today. I thought I would stop by and see how you're doing." Many patients were too sedated, too weak, or in too much pain to talk. Others spoke no English. But many surprised Clare by engaging with her.

Nurses warned her this day that a pneumonia patient on the ward, Forrest, a man she had already met in the emergency room, was verbally abusive, agitated, and disoriented. Donning a face mask, Clare entered Forrest's room and found him tied to his bed by four-point restraints.

Wracked by delirium tremens, raging against his cloth bonds, Forrest nevertheless remembered her and welcomed her like an old friend. He begged her to help him escape, asking her to contact a physician at the hospital, a Dr. Rush, who, Forrest said, would discharge him. He also wanted her to bring him a knife from his backpack.

Clare sat by his bed and leaned down to meet his eyes. "I will do what I can to help you," she said, "on one condition. You have to give me your complete attention for three minutes."

Forrest agreed.

Moving a little closer, her gaze locked on Forrest's, Clare smiled broadly. "You," she whispered conspiratorially to Forrest, "are going to get me in big trouble!" Forrest burst into laughter, and the sound of their mirth filled the room. For Clare, it was a sacred moment of connection, of trust, of vulnerability. She enjoyed a few more moments with Forrest before he slipped back into delirium.

Clare kept her end of the bargain. She opened the backpack, trusting correctly that any knife would have been confiscated by the hospital staff. She also tried to find Dr. Rush, but no one at the hospital knew a doctor by that name. Honoring her promise to Forrest, Clare left a note for "Dr. Rush" at the staff desk anyway.

She left the hospital that day filled with gratitude. "For me, being the loving presence of God for a patient is making that connection. It is a very specific thing. When we make it, it comes with a gasp of recognition. It is always a mutual gift."

A Deepening Spiritual Path. Clare had been a member of her Unitarian church for more than a decade, but her volunteer work as a lay chaplain was a new route to finding her way back to herself. Her midlife crisis drove her to a more profound under-standing of her religious values.

A vibrant, dark-haired woman with a radiant smile, Clare had had a remarkable career. Trained as a Ph.D. economist at the University of California, she had worked on drought relief in Africa with the United Nations. She had spent a few years in her thirties acting professionally in musical theatre; one major theatre critic called her "perfect . . . a sublime blend of face and voice."

In a sharp departure from the arts, Clare eventually became CEO of a management consulting firm that conducted studies for Congress, a creative endeavor that helped reduce government costs without cutting services.

But the last leg of her professional journey, an eight-year

stint as cofounder of a financial services firm, proved so repressive that it sparked a midlife crisis and nearly ruined her health. The start-up was a big success, hitting the *Inc.* 500 list. But Clare lost herself in the pressures of launching, co-owning, and managing marketing and sales.

"I hate selling. I hate it! But what did I do for ten years? I was a front-line marketing and salesperson," she says. "I was good at things that I didn't like to do, and I became captive to my talent."

The ceaseless pressure ground down her joy in life. Struggling for consensus with her partners meant her every creative idea had to be vetted by the group. Disputes over core issues erupted. Over the years, like the proverbial frog in the cookpot who does not realize he is slowly being boiled to death by the ever-hotter water, Clare lost touch with everything in life that mattered to her—her children, her husband, her friends, her body, herself.

By the time she was 50, the pressures had overtaken her health. Once a dancer, Clare developed chronic pain in her neck and lower back and lost all flexibility. She didn't sleep well and constantly had a cold. But "things were piling up so fast and furiously" at work that it did not even occur to her to see a doctor.

One day, before a big marketing presentation on the East Coast, she reached a new low: She could not even fit her feet into her dress shoes. "My feet were swollen, my hands were swollen, my face had broken out," she says. She puzzled over how to jam her swollen feet into the shoes. After the presentation, she spent the return trip throwing up in the airliner's bathroom.

Her friends tried to tell her she was giving away too much of herself to the company—too much time, too much peace of mind. Finally, she quit the firm.

Hungry to reconnect with herself and others, Clare began calling herself "a recovering entrepreneur." Immersed to her elbows in dishwater, talking with another mother at one of her children's camps one day, she learned of a multi-faith chaplaincy program at the county hospital and submitted her application that week.

She told the minister who headed the program that she was looking for an antidote to the ill effects of her decade as a businesswoman. She was craving a more authentic connection with others. "For the past ten years, I started every new relationship I had with an agenda," she told him. "What I'm going to get out of this is the opposite: a creative connection. A healing."

Upon hearing she planned to volunteer, one of her friends "burst into a great hooting laugh and said, 'Well, if I were dying in the hospital, you are the last person I would want to see,'" Clare recalls. Seeing the hurt on her face, he tried to explain that he thought a chaplain should have a calming and subdued presence.

"Let's face it," he told her, "if someone asked me to describe you, 'self-effacing' wouldn't be on the list."

But the program's four-week training program taught Clare ways of connecting with patients under any circumstances. The program assigned her each week to various wards in the city's only public hospital—the psych ward, the AIDS unit, intensive care, the emergency room.

She learned to listen actively, to empathize without passing judgment, to avoid trying to control conversations or to "fix" or change patients. Chaplains in the program were to "accompany the patient on his or her journey, without judgment, with no personal agenda. Chaplains do not proselytize," she was told.

In her ministry, she got back much more than she gave, she discovered. She learned to pray with the emaciated Nigerian woman who had come to the United States for treatment of a rare skin disease, leaving her three small children with her parents. Weeping, she told Clare she never expected to see her husband and babies again.

She comforted a 42-year-old woman with a drug habit who had contracted AIDS five years earlier. Clare listened to her talk for hours amid sobs, about how she had loved her family in Michigan, and how they at first had taken her in to nurse her through her illness. Then, when they learned she had AIDS, they called the police to throw her out. "She spent the night in jail, because there was nowhere else for her to stay," Clare says.

Yet another patient was astonished when Clare took seriously his talk of spirituality. He had admitted himself to the hospital to keep from killing himself, he said. His inner demons would not leave him alone and he could no longer endure their torment. Raised as a churchgoer, he talked with God often. "He was used to being treated like a nut case, and he was flabbergasted that I saw his quest as a spiritual gift. We talked about how he was a loner and had never benefited from time-tested disciplines" of spirituality, Clare says.

Communion with the downtrodden sparked a major insight. "I understand more clearly now," she says, "how much I want to live in authentic relationship" with others, free of any ulterior motives and the distortions of competition.

The Seeker opened the door for a wealth of new pursuits for Clare. The first was to recover from fifteen years of office work by getting fit and enjoying her body again. "I'd moved from being a moderately fit thirty-five-year-old to a very sedentary fifty-year-old," she says.

She signed up for a jazz-blues dance class that became central in her healing. The teacher, a man she has known in her church community for years, inspires students to "trust the music and be in the passion of the music. Dancing is an artistic expression in this class for us all, whatever level we are," Clare says. "I wept after the first class I took. I just wept. I remember thinking, 'Omigod, I have missed this so much. The physicality of it, the expressiveness.'"

The lay chaplaincy combined with the dancing marked a turning point. Thus grounded, "I reclaimed the sense that I could not be captive of things that are not good for me," she says.

Clare created a holiday pageant for her church that was so successful it has become a tradition. Through it, she connected with a group of actors and directors and joined an annual fund-raising production in which she again sang and danced onstage. She has discovered a keen talent for writing and is drafting a play based roughly on women from her dance class. She freelanced as a promoter for an independent filmmaker whose work she admires. She also joined a nonprofit board that furthers arts education in public schools.

Clare is working again now, but midlife crisis has transformed the criteria she establishes for any job. Her current post as a managing director for a nonprofit has her doing work she loves. Now, "I'm much more attuned to how the work feels to me. Am I able to be authentic while doing this? Am I proud of doing this? Does it feel like I'm making a positive contribution? Is it a right thing to do? Does it contribute to a more positive world?" On her current job, all the answers are yes. "All I 'sell' now is good ideas about how to make the world a better place," she says.

If—and only if—work meets these spiritual criteria is Clare willing to give herself over to it.

Many women in my study faced health problems, as Clare did, that helped trigger a midlife crisis. Some underwent not only a change in life direction, but a transformation of their entire philosophy of life. In Kate's case, the Seeker served as a support for such a fundamental change.

The Seeker as Salvation. Kate roared through the first part of her adult life like a speeding train. Riding high on the leading edge of American business, she worked 90-hour weeks as a consultant for a series of innovative firms.

She loved ambiguity, solving complex problems, and slashing

new paths in uncharted territory. She developed new distribution networks, charted new marketing strategies, forged joint ventures among corporate behemoths. In each case she aimed to control all that lay before her. "You're harnessing something that looks like a whirlwind. Your job is to figure out how."

She hopped planes in a heartbeat, traveling five days a week. She and her husband, a corporate sales manager, sometimes lived apart for months at a time. "My husband would tell you my job came first, second, third, fourth, and fifth in my life, and he fell somewhere below that," Kate says. "I had no energy left for marriage. I was consumed by work."

At age 38, Kate's speeding train hit a wall. The surprise news that she was pregnant slowed her pace, then forced her to go on bedrest at her Illinois home. She and her husband had earlier tried conceiving children but failed and gave up. As they struggled to adjust, the birth of twins led Kate to drop out of the workforce.

Shortly thereafter she and her husband suffered a series of losses: One of their baby daughters was diagnosed with a disability. Her husband's father died. Kate's mother received a cancer diagnosis. In turmoil himself, Kate's husband separated from her for six months, then moved back in. In a final blow, Kate was diagnosed with multiple sclerosis, a disease that is not disabling at this point, but which could become so.

Struggling to cope, Kate turned a critical eye on her past. The cancer that beset her mother, whose "Energizer Bunny" approach to life is very similar to Kate's, led Kate to question her own type-A pace. She spent time in therapy looking at how her lifestyle had affected her marriage, and questioning her priorities. "Is running from job to job because it's cool and exciting, the best thing for anyone to do? I don't think it was healthy for the marriage, and I think it was very self-absorbed," Kate says.

Kate had never seen herself as a spiritual person. When her parents signed her up for confirmation classes in their church at age 12, she struck a bargain with them: "I don't believe in God, so I don't feel a need to be confirmed," she told them. Her parents agreed that she was free to make that choice, but only after she had taken a full series of confirmation classes. "I took the classes and I said at the end, 'This didn't change my mind.' So I didn't have to join the church."

It took a midlife crisis to jolt her onto a different path. On the advice of a friend, Kate took up meditation and began reading spiritual works by Buddhist monk Thich Nhat Hanh and others. With her two three-year-olds, she practices walking meditation. She is training herself to avoid getting mired in attempts to control the people and things around her, "pushing and pulling at things to try to get them to fit the way I think they should be," she says.

In contrast with her past, "this is definitely a spiritual journey for me," Kate says. She sees "some karmic forces that have been trying to get me to focus on what's important, and I have never paid attention to them." The birth of twins, the marital upheaval, the health problems—all, Kate concluded, were part of a larger plan to shake her up, to force her to be more healthy in the way she lives, to give up trying to control everything.

All this has helped her slow down and savor each moment. "I'm feeling more of a smoothness" of mind, she says. "My goal is to be able to live comfortably with chaos."

Her spiritual studies have helped her to better understand her husband, a practicing Taoist. And it has given rise to a new set of hopes for her future: She wants healthy, happy kids. She hopes to raise them with a more balanced, healthier lifestyle than the one she embraced in her youth. And for herself, "I hope I can continue down a path of being more comfortable with myself and more comfortable with what's happening next," Kate says, "and to let things . . . to let things go, to take things as they happen and be happy with that."

While Kate's midlife crisis led her to a more contemplative mode of living, the Seeker's transformative energy also can splinter into secular pursuits. Molly's story shows what can happen when a deeply spiritual woman seeks secular paths out of midlife crisis.

Suppressing the Seeker. For as long as she can remember, Molly dreamed of leading a monastic life. She wanted to be a nun from the time she entered a Catholic elementary school in Illinois. In a photo of her grade-school graduation, she is holding a nun doll. "I wanted to be a saint or a martyr, and give my life to the Church," she says. In a playground game called "Going to Heaven, Going to Hell," she played Saint Michael, saving playmates from demons seeking to tear them limb from limb.

A middle child in a large family, Molly became a caregiver at an early age, watching out for a younger brother with Down syndrome, protecting him and making sure no one ever made fun of him or hurt him. "We were raised to feel it was our duty to make sure nobody was ever treated unfairly because of their disability," says Molly. Thus began her lifelong role as champion of the downtrodden.

A bout with rheumatic fever at age nine confined her to her room for months, accustoming her to solitude. "I had to sit and watch everybody else play and go to school. I was an observer for a whole year. It made a huge impression on me," she says. Molly grew into adolescence determined to fulfill her dream of becoming a nun. But in the first of what would be several similar decisions in her life, Molly set aside her spiritual aspirations and heeded adults' advice to enter teaching instead.

Her choices in young adulthood kept her on a different spiritual path. A tall, beautiful blond woman with deep-set eyes, she was drawn in college to John, a man who lived the role of a spiritual teacher in iconoclastic 1970s style. Charismatic and well-read, John held forth in the student union at Molly's university on topics ranging from philosophy to the *I Ching*. Students gathered around him to listen. Molly was irresistibly drawn: "I felt I was fated to be with this guy." He taught her Greek and they read the Great Books together and studied the original text of the New Testament.

Their relationship, oddly, remained celibate. Molly would later learn that John was gay. But the sexual gulf between them mattered less to her than the spiritual togetherness they shared, and John remained her partner for twenty-two years. Molly had never wanted marriage and children anyway, she says. "I think I felt called to take care of the whole world, rather than taking care of a small family."

Her relationship with John gave her something "very different from what most women get. It fed my soul," she says. "After a while the sexual thing didn't matter. I had always wanted to be a nun. And here I was with this deeply spiritual person with whom I had conversations about Plato's ideas, about philosophical and spiritual things."

She taught school briefly, then she and John moved to California where Molly, with John's encouragement and support, landed a series of ever-higher-paying corporate jobs. As a couple, they cofounded a successful consulting business. Molly learned to handle herself in the most intimidating business situations, going nose-to-nose with CEOs to make deals and manage client relationships. John joined the Catholic Church and became a deacon. Together, they ministered part-time to the sick and dying in a big urban hospital.

Molly's midlife crisis began at age 41, with John's premature death from cancer. For a year Molly was consumed with his care. Wracked with pain, John was often awake and kept the light on through the night; Molly stayed by his side, sleeping little. In his final stage of life at the hospital, Molly stayed overnight so often that the staff thought she was a private-duty nurse. She bought tombstones at a two-for-one sale and had her own name carved on the other marker.

As Molly grieved John's impending death, her dream of becoming a nun surfaced again in her thoughts. She yearned to join a Carmelite monastery near her city. Sometimes she would visit the community of fifteen nuns and sit, listening to their singing and contemplating what her life there might be like.

But again, Molly was dissuaded. In their many talks anticipating the afterlife, John assured her, "I'll be watching out for you."

"I think I'm going to become a Carmelite. I want to be a cloistered nun," Molly told him.

"That's very interesting. But don't do anything drastic for at least a year," John advised her. "Don't move away. Don't become a nun. Just try to keep up with what you're doing for a while. Continue your business."

Molly felt frustrated. She had plenty of savings from her many years of hard work. But she promised John she would do as he advised. She oversaw a huge funeral at their cathedral, with bishops presiding and hundreds of people in attendance, from homeless people John had helped to high-ranking officials of the church. In keeping with his life, the rituals around John's death were marked by a mystical event.

A homeless woman entered the cathedral during the wake, fell weeping to her knees before John's casket, and began to pray. When Molly approached her to comfort her, she explained that she had been standing at the edge of a highway nearby, preparing to commit suicide by rushing into traffic. She was drawn to the cathedral and saw a vision, she said, of a face, a bearded man with long hair who looked like Jesus, speaking to her encouragingly and reassuring her that all would be okay.

The image looked exactly like John.

Midlife Meltdown. With John's powerful influence removed, Molly's repressed dreams and desires began to resurface with blinding force. She kept her promise to John, staying the course in her business for a year, then shutting it down to take a corporate job in a key staff position for a big company.

But in all other realms her energies fragmented, flickering wildly like light through a prism. She found some letters from an old high school boyfriend who still lived near her Illinois hometown. Mustering her courage, she called him during a Thanksgiving visit home and they tumbled headlong into a passionate love affair.

For Molly, it was like picking up an intriguing novel she had laid down, unfinished, two decades ago. "To have someone interested in me sexually. . . . I thought I was about to explode," she says. "It reawakened everything in me that had not had any expression for twenty years." She wrote pages and pages of poetry about her love, then an entire novel. Her lover told her she had not changed; she fantasized about him constantly. "It was like living in a fairy tale."

The transcontinental relationship soon crumbled, however, under the weight of the lovers' mutual projections. In her delight Molly had seen only what she wanted to see in her old friend—glossing over their many incompatibilities. As painful as was the breakup, "getting back into those girl feelings was very important to my rejuvenation. The idea of romance, even if it doesn't work out, is very hopeful. And hope is important," Molly says.

Molly plunged into other pursuits. Sitting with friends at

some of the same open-mike coffeehouses where Beat poet Allen Ginsberg made his name, she would screw up her courage and stand to read her poetry. To be heard and praised for her work was exhilarating.

Her midlife crisis had its comic moments. Inspired by a friend's love for motorcycles, Molly bought her own Harley, a hulking 880-cc Sportster, got her license, donned her boots, helmet, and goggles, hopped aboard, and pulled out of the driveway. The 500-pound bike promptly fell over and landed on her foot, opening a puncture wound big enough to require a tetanus shot. A friend rescued her and schooled her in an empty lot until she mastered the fine points of motorcycling.

She joined a club, the Fog Hogs, and toured the California countryside with groups of twenty fellow bikers. She had thought motorcycling would help her meet lots of interesting men in midlife crisis—the Harley-riding doctors and lawyers she had read about in the newspapers. She was disappointed to find herself riding with what she regarded as grizzled old hillbillies—men who chewed tobacco and spent rest stops spitting the juice. "Hanging out with them would be like kissing an ashtray," Molly lamented. "I never saw any of those professionals I'd read about."

Staving Off Loneliness. When her beloved mother died a year after John, Molly grew angrier at this second loss. She took up yet another venture, as a patron and performer with a local theatre group. "I was hanging out with crazy people, staying out all night. I was kind of out of control," she says. She filled her life with younger friends to try to cope with loneliness.

She began seeing a psychiatrist at a friend's insistence and started the hard work of resolving her losses. "One of the main lessons of midlife crisis is that you can't be afraid to be alone, to be alone with your thoughts," she says.

Meanwhile, the currents of life continued to sweep Molly further from her dream of monastic life. She took the law school entrance exams on a lark. A friend showed her a pamphlet on preparatory exams and they agreed, "Let's do that!" Molly says. "We showed up and I got this incredibly high score." Her company agreed to pay half her tuition and she enrolled and earned a law degree.

At work, she met a lawyer on a case for her company, a conservative, Ivy League–educated easterner who was "hysterically funny." Molly invited him out and began dating him. Their sex life at first was white-hot.

"He thought we should get married. 'Why not?' I said. 'I haven't done that before.'" But Molly realized almost immediately that marriage imposed constraints she did not like. Five years later, their sexual edge has mellowed, but they are working hard to sustain a shared life. "I can't believe I got married," she says. Looking back, she wishes they had decided instead to just live together, an arrangement that would have done less damage to her sense of independence.

As Molly progresses through her midlife crisis, she says, "I keep being reminded that I've got a mind and a spirit that have become so much more important to me than my body." She still yearns to fulfill a different dream, one she has deferred, of founding a retreat center for others to use as a sanctuary for spiritual and creative renewal.

What would have happened if Molly had followed her original dream and become a Carmelite nun? She hedges, saying she does not want to sound egotistical. At my urging, she tells me that her years of suffering, grieving for John and her mother, doing battle with CEOs, experiencing the disappointments of life, have made her tough. Thus tempered, Molly believes she would bring great strength to a monastic existence.

"Whatever intensity I've got inside me that keeps all these flames burning would probably have turned me into some kind of visionary," she says.

Looking back over her midlife decisions, Molly is reminded of an Arthurian legend about the magician Merlin, as told by author Mary Stewart in a series of books. Frustrated as a young man by his inability to fall in love, Merlin seeks counsel and is told to be satisfied with the powerful gift he has been given, as a sorcerer. Perhaps, says Molly, the lesson in her experience is the same: "The gods only give one gift at a time."

Tracking the Seeker. Molly received no encouragement to live a religious life. Instead, loved ones repeatedly erected roadblocks against her interest in monasticism. Had Molly allowed the Seeker within to emerge more fully at midlife, she might have taken a different path.

There are few marked paths in today's culture for women guided by the Seeker. By conventional yardsticks, participation is declining in religion—defined as an institutionalized system of attitudes, beliefs, and practices shaping one's relationship with God or the divine. The proportion of Americans reporting they are connected with no established religion at all has grown to about 14 percent from 9 percent just a decade ago.[12]

However, the established-religion yardstick misses much of what women in my study regarded as spirituality—that is, the state of being dedicated to God, the divine, or spiritual or sacred values, as opposed to material or secular ones. Many women said they measure their own spirituality by personal encounters with God or a higher power, or by a belief in a larger or divine truth. Their experiences range from sensing contact or oneness with a sacred being to seeking enlightenment or some other form of religious or mystical experience. Some find religious meaning in social and environmental activism, as Clare did.

Midlife crisis distilled these spiritual yearnings for many women, igniting a spiritual spark for the first time. "I don't know that God ever talked to me for the first forty-two years, but for the last two years we've had a continual dialogue," says Hilary, a Colorado executive, echoing the experience of others.

A significant minority of women in my study described being deeply affected at some point by some kind of religious or spiritual experience or voice. Beyond classical works in Buddhism, Taoism, and other Eastern religions, some cited such works as *The Celestine Prophecy* by James Redfield, with its theme that mystical guidance is accessible in everyday life, or Thomas Moore's *Dark Nights of the Soul*, with its emphasis on the spiritual importance of life's crisis moments, as examples of books that have proven important.

Until better measures are developed for Americans' contemporary religious experiences, no one will know exactly how powerful a role the Seeker is playing in shaping this generation of women. But if my study is any guide, it is a powerful role indeed.

Part III

✦ ✦ ✦

REACHING OUT
AT MIDLIFE

9

◆ ◆ ◆

SHARING OUR WISDOM

Those who cannot learn from history are doomed
to repeat it.

— GEORGE SANTAYANA

One of the damnable realities of midlife crisis is that you cannot see what is happening to you because you are drowning in emotional white water. Distinguishing between personal growth and the path to perdition can be nearly impossible.

Yet much is at stake. The way a woman navigates midlife crisis has a profound effect on the quality of her life in old age. Her success in reintegrating the lost archetypes of midlife crisis shapes her chances of finding peace and fulfillment in her later years. Each of the archetypes, based on several long-term landmark studies of aging, corresponds with specific traits and behaviors that are known to improve a woman's health and well-being late in life.

Thus we stand to learn much from midlife crisis. Yet contemporary culture affords no customary, established way of sharing, woman to woman, mother to daughter, parent to child, the wisdom we acquire in this crucible. Instead, most women feel more isolated at this stage. Nearly every woman in my study believed she was alone in her midlife turmoil, despite abundant evidence to the contrary.

Placing higher value on storytelling is one way to avert that isolation. Merely gathering the stories I have retold in this book transformed my own view of the vast creative and generative potential of this life stage. This chapter shares the stories of four veterans of midlife crisis who have progressed into old age and can share the wisdom of hindsight on choices they made at midlife.

Creating new, systematic ways of gathering together to share our stories is another antidote to isolation. This chapter makes a case for creating organized groups and retreats, for the purpose of passing on more of the wisdom born of midlife turmoil.

A Formula for Well-Being. By integrating the archetypes of midlife crisis, a woman can bring forth particular attributes associated with a long and happy life, as identified by four landmark studies of aging: the so-called Nun Study, of 678 Catholic sisters; the MacArthur Foundation Study of Successful Aging; the Harvard Study of Adult Development; and a twelve-year study by William Sadler, a business and sociology professor at Holy Names College in Oakland, California. Some of these traits and behaviors, and their relationship to the archetypes, are described in more detail in Appendix C.

Many benefits are fairly straightforward. The Lover develops the more intimate relationships and the deep caring for others that are linked to well-being in old age. The Leader fosters the risk taking, autonomy, and initiative associated with healthy aging, and may also lead to more meaningful work.

The Adventurer builds physical fitness, an openness to new ideas and experiences, and the capacity for joy and play that keep us young. The Artist also explores our capacity for joy and play, as well as autonomy, connection with community, and the ability to engage in meaningful work. The Gardener fosters connection with community, as well as concern for others, an ability to derive enjoyment from past accomplishments, and a deep caring for others and the earth. Finally, the Seeker builds the deep spirituality, openness to new ideas, optimism, and hope that have been linked to well-being among the very old.

Learning from Our Stories. Stories from others' lives can be invaluable in understanding how and why archetypes emerge in us. Storytelling is uniquely suited to passing on the wisdom gleaned from midlife crisis. It allows us to communicate unspoken knowledge that might otherwise be difficult to pass on. Because we can convey emotion in our stories, we can also transmit layers of meaning beyond our words. And storytelling affords living examples of how to handle a challenge, showing others, rather than telling them, how to live.

When women learn from each other's stories, says Melanie, profiled in chapter 7, "it's like passing on a recipe to somebody else. At any given moment, that same recipe may be being put together in Chicago or Portland, by some other woman. It's a hope we all have—that some essence of our being will have an impact somewhere."

To capture a few complete stories of midlife crisis, viewed through the clarifying lens of hindsight, I sought out several older women in their late fifties, sixties, and seventies who had experienced midlife crises a decade or more ago. I asked them how their midlife decisions had shaped their experience in old age, and what they would do differently if they could.

Without exception, the women who made big midlife changes said that if given the chance to do it all again, they would embrace new undertakings even more wholeheartedly. Every one of the women who entered fully into midlife crisis, taking risks and exploring new opportunities, was enthusiastically glad that she had. Their only regrets were in failing to start sooner or to take more chances.

At the least, each of these women reaped memories that sustained her for years. Amanda left her career as a math professor at forty-three to return to college as a Ph.D. candidate, then pursued a lifelong dream of re-creating the copper-red glazes of China's Sung dynasty. Her work with ceramics led her to make pioneering discoveries on the structure of certain mineral forms. That work is a bulwark of her sense of personal identity.

Now 64, Amanda still revels in those memories. "Whenever I feel sad, I look back at that," she says. "People who climb Mount Everest climb it once. You don't expect to spend your whole life eating magic mushrooms. You don't expect to spend your entire life communing with God.

"I had my God Moment," Amanda says, "and it was enough."

The only overwhelming regrets I found were among the Non-Starters—the women whose fears had prevented them from making changes.

The biggest mistake, it seems, is not having a midlife crisis at all.

An Entirely New Life. Marilyn's midlife crisis at age 48 yielded so many rewarding changes in her life that, at 71, she can hardly wait to get out of bed in the morning.

It all began with a self-discovery seminar of a kind popular in the 1970s, EST. Marilyn had been married for thirty years by then to her junior high school sweetheart, a man who expected his wife to tend home and hearth. Trained from childhood to be positive and eschew anger at all costs, Marilyn grew up pretending she liked things she did not, to please others. She acted out the role of an ever-happy housewife for years. Outside the home, her work was confined to community nonprofits.

The role fell far short of satisfying her. In her restlessness, she had an extramarital affair. "I was like a horse straining at the reins all the time."

The EST seminar, suggested by one of her college-age children, jolted her into a new honesty. "I saw myself as if I was standing in front of a circular mirror, viewing myself from all directions. It was as if I suddenly took off the dark glasses." She found the courage to reveal her discontent to her husband and tell him about her affair. They soon divorced.

A lifelong acrophobe, Marilyn signed on for wilderness training.

In a life-changing move called a Tyrolean Traverse, she rode a zipline from a mountain peak to the ground hundreds of feet below. "I stood on the edge of a cliff with tears pouring down my face. And I shut my eyes and went down, screaming with joy at the top of my lungs. I was so exhilarated.

"Once you do that, you see that fear is always present," but it need not be paralyzing, she says. In any potentially intimidating endeavor, "you can just include your fear and keep going."

She began exploring another dream. "I had always felt I was an entrepreneur. Give me a whiteboard and I'll write something on it," she says. So she sold her house and plowed everything she had into founding a business. "Picking up the phone and asking somebody to try what you have to offer? It's the zipline all over again," she says. She grew her consulting business into a respected, leading position in her field.

In her mid-fifties, after dating various men and "kissing a lot of frogs," Marilyn resolved to find a mate. Years before the era of Internet dating, she mustered her courage and placed a newspaper ad:

DWF. Bright, pretty, petite, dark-haired, young mid-50s, healthy, interested and passionate in life and love. Seeking warm, bright, classy, emotionally and financially secure man to share life, fun & romance.

Baring her heart in black-and-white was like jumping off the zipline all over again. Gamblers, drinkers, men with whom she had nothing in common, soon filled her mailbox with replies. Last to respond was her next husband, a man in his sixties. The first evening he arrived at her door to pick her up, Marilyn says, they knew they wanted to be together.

Asked about her second marriage, Marilyn sighs. "It's amazing, just amazing. My husband . . . has all the qualities I am missing. When I married him, I said, 'This is like coming home for me. I have found my missing piece.'"

Every day now, Marilyn enjoys the fruits of her midlife crisis. "I've had two complete and total lives," she says. "One was based on just putting one foot in front of the other. The other life began at forty-eight, and it was totally committed, disciplined, with complete integrity, doing what I said I would do." And that, for this lifetime, has been enough.

Marilyn's only regret is failing to start sooner. "If I had to redesign my life, I would have started at a very early age to do what I said I would do, and to strive for authenticity," she says. If she had, Marilyn believes, her midlife crisis would not have been such an explosive affair.

Finding What You Love. At age 79, Sharon savors a wealth of memories, many of them accumulated during a rip-roaring midlife crisis. Looking back, the Connecticut mother of two is glad she had one, and glad she preserved her marriage throughout. Today, she and her husband have been married for more than a half-century.

By nature an Adventurer, Sharon gained a college education,

an ability to take risks, a positive sense of personal identity, and a career as an archaeologist. The advice she would offer younger women: Find something you truly love—and do it.

For her first five decades of life, Sharon was a devoted wife and mother, but did not find any other work she enjoyed. She had never attended college and was pained by that fact. She had worked only in secretarial and administrative jobs. She met her husband, a traveling international executive, in South Africa where she grew up, married him later in Europe, and moved with him to the United States in the 1960s. They raised two successful children, with Sharon playing the corporate-wife role to perfection.

But Sharon felt diminished when her husband's business associates looked right through her at dinner parties. When she offered an opinion to her table partners at one gathering, a drunken associate of her husband's retorted, "Who gives a fuck what you think?"

Her transformation began one day in 1976. Her two children had left for college. She was sitting in a restaurant with her husband, by then the CEO of an international company, her mind drifting as he talked shop with an associate.

Bored, she looked ceilingward and began to count the light fixtures. "One, two, three . . . What am I doing?" she wondered with an edge of desperation.

Her gaze drifted out the window and alighted on the entrance sign to Hunter College. Abandoning the lunch group, she jumped up and trotted over to pick up an application.

Thus began Sharon's Sonic Boom. Her enrollment at age 50

as one of Hunter's oldest students marked the beginning of a great adventure that would transform her from a stay-at-home wife with an empty nest into an archaeologist traversing Middle Eastern minefields and probing the mysteries of the Nile.

Oh, the Places You'll Go! Traveling with a colleague, Sharon took several three-month research expeditions to Egypt. Her team visited the Springs of Moses, where the prophet was said to have drawn water from rock with a blow from his staff. As they walked, Egyptian soldiers fired their weapons in warning— they were stepping through a live minefield! "Fools rush in," Sharon says, and chuckles. "I had no idea what I was getting into." Her driver later told them a truck had been blown up there just weeks earlier.

She also had no idea she would become so passionately interested in archaeology. Told a particular site, a mountaintop shrine where the ancient Egyptians had prayed to their gods four thousand years earlier, was only reachable by helicopter, Sharon and her team climbed to it on foot. "We didn't have a helicopter," she says simply.

She slept in the Sinai in a tent zipped tight against cobras and scorpions. Mistaken for heroin smugglers, she and her team were nearly arrested. Sharon dropped ten pounds climbing the cliffs along the Nile and probing deep tomb shafts for information. "I'd never been in better shape," she says. She finished her degree with a 4.0 grade average and made Phi Beta Kappa.

At last, Sharon felt "adequate." She says, "My whole world

changed for the better. Archaeology filled an enormous void in my life. It gave me an amazing sense of independence. And it gave me my own identity."

In seeking out what to do at midlife, Sharon advises, do not worry too much about what that something is. Just make sure that you truly love it. At age 79, she still abides by what she learned as an Adventurer: "It doesn't really matter where you go. It always leads to another place."

Take More Risks. Looking back, Eleanor, at age 71, says her crisis in her early forties greatly enriched her life. The California paralegal found a meaningful sideline career at midlife, as a screenwriter. Her midlife crisis also strengthened her capacity for joy and play, her ability to take risks, and her sense of personal identity.

Eleanor has only one regret: She wishes she had taken even more chances. Had she been a little more daring, risked a little more money, time, and security, she might have had even more fun and more colorful memories to enjoy.

Her transformation began in a sunlit moment at age 40, when Eleanor experienced the essence of midlife crisis—"that fleeting bit of time when everything felt possible again."

Racing along near a Pacific Ocean beach on a bicycle with coworkers on an office outing, the sunshine kindled in Eleanor some long-lost sense of immortality. She pedaled faster, faster, pulling in front of her younger friends until she was speeding wildly over the sand.

"I can still feel that sense of exhilaration—head of the pack—the sun—the wind—the ocean smell there, near the beach. It was a moment of madness," Eleanor says. "From childhood, some remembered ride down a hill at breakneck speed seemed distinctly possible."

Until it wasn't. Eleanor's front tire hit a stone, which pitched her headfirst onto the sand and knocked her senseless. Next came an ambulance ride to the local emergency room, and treatment for a minor concussion.

Paradoxically, the crash gave her courage. "I felt a little more secure in myself. It gave me confidence," she says. When a mugger later tried to attack her, she stood her ground and screamed—an act of defiance she believes she could not have managed before her accident. Her would-be assailant ran away.

The bike crash also allowed her inner Artist onto center stage. Raised in a tiny rural Missouri town Eleanor describes as "the size of a pencil eraser," she married young, to a high school classmate, and had three children. They divorced, and for years Eleanor dedicated herself to raising her kids.

By her forties, Eleanor began a restrained, Moderate-mode transformation. She screwed up her courage to enroll in an evening screenwriting class at UCLA. Eleanor lacked a college degree. But as a child she had loved to sing, perform, and make people laugh, and she had always loved to write.

To her surprise and delight, the teacher liked her work so much that he invited her to join a small, elite group of students in his private writing workshop, where Eleanor polished and perfected her craft for years. In her scripts, her characters always seem to change. But, in fact, "they not so much change as rediscover the people they were," she says.

Eleanor's midlife crisis has followed the same theme. She has learned "to feel confident of your inner core. The things that defined you as a child probably will carry you through the hard times." Whatever mishaps befall you, "nobody can really hurt you as long as you have the courage to be who you are."

That lesson, Eleanor says, frames her only regret—that she had not been more adventurous in earlier years. She recalls a road trip from the past, one of many she took as a single mom with her children. The family had left early one morning and secured a campsite on a beautiful California lake. As soon as they settled in, her children began begging Eleanor to rent a rowboat to explore the lake. The cost was $8 a day.

Eleanor was always pressed for cash; it was not easy to raise three children alone on a paralegal's salary. "I don't think I can afford it," she told the children, and stuck to her position over their begging. Looking back, Eleanor wishes she had rented the boat. "We could have eaten beans the next week" to cover the cost, she says now.

Her children do not even remember the incident. But "that $8 boat has stayed on the top of my consciousness, and it always makes me 'go for it' now," she says.

The Right Response. Asked what principles helped her navigate midlife crisis so well, Eleanor tells a story from her childhood. She was ten years old, playing after a Sunday night church service in her small Missouri town. Churchgoers were gathered talking, when a new set of headlights swept the church-yard. A knock on the door followed. A stranger entered the room and began to speak.

He needed money, he told the congregants. He had fallen on hard times and needed to buy milk for his baby, food for his family.

The people of the church looked at each other, then passed a hat and collected among them about $50. The man took the money, thanked them, and drove away.

He was probably a con artist, one man said. Others mur-mured agreement.

Eleanor's father spoke up. "Well, you know, maybe he was," he said. "But the thing we decided to do is the thing we have to measure ourselves by. Maybe he did need the money, maybe he didn't. We'll never know. But what we will know is that we did the right thing."

In tough times, Eleanor says, she has called the story to mind. It reminds her that no one is immune from the losses and blows of midlife. A hurricane of blows will inevitably rain down upon you—death, disease, despair, disappointment, an empty nest, an empty bed, the loneliness and decay of aging. It also may bring liberations, such as an inheritance or freedom from old responsibilities. No one can control these circumstances.

What shapes our lives in old age is not the losses, but how we respond. The story reminds her, Eleanor says, that "nobody or nothing can really hurt you, as long as you have the courage to be who you are."

Marching in Place. As mentioned earlier in this chapter, the biggest mistake may be in not having a midlife crisis at all. Many women—roughly 64 percent, based upon the MacArthur Foundation research discussed in chapter 1—do not have what they regard as a midlife crisis. Many do not feel the need. But others resist repressed passions or desires.

Looking back, Kay, at nearly 60, a freelance consultant from New York, wishes she had found a way to break through the fears that held her back in her forties. She wishes she had been more outgoing, built more skills, and taken more career risks.

She did make some attempts to engage in new pursuits, joining a chorus and enrolling in religious studies and astronomy classes. But depression and anxiety proved too-tall obstacles, rooted deep in an unhappy childhood that included emotional abuse by her parents. To Kay's disappointment, they also refused to send her to college. A great beauty in her youth, with big wide-set eyes accented by high, defined cheekbones, perfect skin, and a mass of dark curly hair, Kay married at 18 and was happy for a while. But her husband gradually descended into addiction and mental illness, and she divorced him when she was 32.

Now, she wishes she had some new passion to sustain her through old age. "I don't, and I really feel the lack of it," she says. "I just have this constant, ever-present anxiety about what's going to happen to me tomorrow. And that anxiety just keeps me paralyzed, rooted to the spot, in constant fear and constant worry."

Aging is forcing her to let go of youthful standards of beauty. After midlife, "you will never look young again. Forget it," she says curtly. Unlike some women in my study, she believes it is simply too late to embark on a second life. "I'm not going now to go to college to get my B.A. and start a career as a biochemist. There's no time."

As a result, "I stay in the same emotional place, where everybody around me is growing, changing, doing things," she says. "I feel crushed by the life I've ended up with."

The Need for Sharing. Isolation marked the emotional lives of every single woman in my study who felt her midlife crisis had turned out badly. Some had carried out affairs or adventures in secret, and others had for some reason withheld information from friends about their emotional turbulence. Arguably, isolation contributed to their disappointment, by preventing them from gaining new perspectives or receiving emotional support.

Evidence is growing of the importance of friendships and networks of caring relationships to mental and physical health. Several studies have found that maintaining a connection with community—membership in social groups and regular contact with family and friends—reduces the risk of death and increases well-being in old age. Women who have a circle of female friends report higher well-being than women who lack such a group. Those who are close to their friends also report less depression and higher morale.[1]

A few of the women in my study built reliable, organized, or semi-structured groups of friends into their lives, helping each other through all kinds of midlife challenges. Helena, the artist in chapter 6, has a group of midlife women friends who call themselves the "sorority sisters" and consider themselves even closer than birth sisters. The group helped Helena move to a tiny apartment post-divorce, then pooled some cash to pay painters to brighten it up. Later, the same friends helped renovate the old house she bought. Helena and others also nursed one of their friends after a bad accident.

At a Christmas party Helena held for the group, her teenage daughter said, "This is Mama's tribe. I hope when I grow up, I can have a tribe even half this interesting."

Clare, the executive from California profiled in chapter 8, found her tribe in a twice-weekly modern dance class. Joining in enjoyment of the music, strengthening their bodies, loving the music, brought the women in the class so close that Clare is writing a musical based on the lives of her classmates. The dance class, she says, has become "a little community" for her.

Another kind of connection is forged by women members of "The Women's Circle," a series of retreats and standing support groups for women organized by two Evanston, Illinois, psychotherapists. Participants, most of them in their late thirties to late forties, meet at a wooded camp in Wisconsin to tell their stories of transition. Women's Circle enrollees also are assigned a "co-madre," a practice in Mexican culture that affords each child two mothers—her birth mother and another older woman who remains deeply involved and available to her for life. Support groups are formed among participants and continue to meet regularly after the retreats.

The goal: to build a new relationship with themselves, and to learn from each other's stories. "There's something so powerful about telling your story and having people be able to listen to you—to just be heard," says Wendy Kopald, one of the psychotherapists who founded the program. At midlife, practicing new ways of relating to others and expressing oneself in a group of supportive women can aid personal growth.

A handful of New York women deliberately organized a group for this purpose; it meets bimonthly to help members realize their midlife dreams. It is an example worth emulating.

A Salon of Dreams. Dining with a dozen close friends around a big table at a Manhattan restaurant one evening in 1996, Amy Greenberg decided to try out a new idea.

The women were mostly in their forties and fifties, and many were going through midlife transitions. "It was a time in our lives when we were thinking, 'What else is there?'" says Leslie Rutkin, one of the friends. The waiter had brought coffee and the dinner was winding to a close. Enjoying the warmth and companionship, Greenberg spoke up.

"Why don't we go around the table and everybody just say a dream? Something that you've quietly thought about, and that you've been keeping under wraps—something that you've been quietly holding dear to yourself, but haven't really talked about with anybody."

"The idea touched a chord in all of us," says Rutkin, who, like the other salon members whose actual full names are used here, was not part of my study. The conversation was the genesis of an ongoing discussion group, "The All Grrrls' Dream Salon," that has continued to meet bimonthly ever since in Greenberg's Manhattan apartment, for the sole purpose of airing, discussing, and supporting each other's midlife dreams.

Greenberg, who had never before allowed herself to be called "a girl," chose the name. "That's 'Grrrls',—as in 'growl.' It's powerful," says Greenberg, who is now 54. "It's this idea of being a female, fierce, exciting, adventurous, lively, passionate— a tigress."

Counting a fabric designer, a writer, a sales rep, a banking executive, a marketing consultant, a literary agent, and a trade association executive among its members, the salon has birthed many dreams into reality. With one another's support, members have founded businesses, created artwork, written books, found new markets for their products, and laid new plans for the future.

Salon ground rules allow each woman fifteen minutes to describe her dream, then each of the other women responds. Only positive responses are allowed—no criticism, sarcasm, ridicule, or disrespect allowed, no matter how flimsy the dream. "This is a supportive, loving, embracing atmosphere," Greenberg says.

Rutkin says, "For me, it was a place where I could voice the unvoiceable, and not have somebody say to me, 'Why?' Instead, the response we always get is, 'That's a really good idea,' or, 'How can we help?'" Even if the dream is sketchy or hare-brained, members get a positive response, such as "That sounds like something really important to you. Let's try looking at it from a different direction and see if we can find a way to make it happen."

"We have recurring dreams, ongoing dreams, way-out dreams," adds salon member Anna Lieber, who owns and runs a marketing consulting business. Any dream is safe: "It's not 'sex in the city.' It's 'sanctuary in the city.'" An avid collector of antique tableware and porcelain, Lieber was helped by salon discussions to begin selling her wares at flea markets.

The group helped Rutkin field a floral-collage business and write a long-planned book, a memoir based on letters between her and her husband during a hard time. Hearing Rutkin reading aloud from her manuscript at a salon meeting moved members to tears, Lieber recalls.

The group encouraged Greenberg, who has been a writer, actor, acting teacher, and founder and owner of a public relations company, to pursue her dream of writing a book on how women in diverse cultures experience menopause. She traveled the country with another salon member for her research, discovering "a kind of happiness I had never known," she says.

Unlike any other place in the world, Greenberg says, the salon is a place where middle-aged women feel proud to have dreams.

In her case, the Dream Salon has enabled her to make a

major investment of herself in helping the next generation. Encouraged again by the group, Greenberg is pursuing a new dream of heading a program for autistic children. She has nearly completed a master's degree in education, and is already teaching children with special needs.

10

✦ ✦ ✦

ACROSS THE GENERATIONS

In the midst of winter, I finally learned that there
was in me an invincible summer.

—ALBERT CAMUS

Driving to her job as an aide in an adult foster home near Portland, Oregon, one summer morning, Kathleen Imel, 51, was thinking about the workday ahead. Five feet five inches tall, with a gentle demeanor, luminous blue eyes, and soft gray curls framing her face, Imel was well trained to care for her troubled and volatile patients.

Then, wheeling around a street corner in her van, Imel saw a scene that horrified her. Two snarling pit bulls were racing toward three people standing in the street. Imel knew dogs, and these two were bearing down to attack. A hope crossed her mind, that the people would hold their ground. If they did, the dogs would run past them and keep going.

"Oh my God," Imel exclaimed. To her horror, a small boy split from the group and tried to flee. "That baby is running!"

She wheeled her van into a driveway, shoved the gearshift into Park, and leapt out, screaming, "Don't run!"

It was too late. The dogs overtook the child, jumped on him, and began nipping, knocking him to the ground, tearing at his head and back. The little boy's cries pierced the air. "Help me! Please just help me!"

Imel raced to the boy and kicked at the dogs. The 60-pound pit bull and his smaller mate ignored her blows and tore at the child's head and arms. She dragged the little boy away but the dogs circled and attacked him again. Kicks, blows with her fists, forceful commands—nothing worked. Doors opened along the street and people came out of their houses. No one moved to help.

Desperate, Imel played her final card, throwing herself on top of the boy, covering his bloody body with hers. "They wanted him and I wasn't going to let them get him," she says. "My body took over. My body simply took over."

The pit bulls jumped on Imel and began tearing at her arms and face, opening deep gashes in their frustrated attempt to get at their prey. Imel reached up and grabbed the bigger dog by the neck, digging her fingers into its jugular.

"NO! GO HOME!" she yelled. The pit bull bit her in the face, tearing off her eyebrow and slashing her eyelid. Blood filled her eye and Imel thought he had bitten it out. A rush of memories flooded her mind, including thoughts of an old friend who had lost an eye.

"Is this what really happens when you die?" she wondered, as the dogs continued to tear at her in a frustrated frenzy. The bigger dog locked on her arm.

Finally, a woman stepped forward and pulled the child from beneath Imel. The dogs still did not let up. Another thought, of the San Francisco woman killed by dogs in her apartment building, entered Imel's mind: "Oh, how horrid it must have been for her." She struggled to hold on to consciousness.

"If I'm going to die," she thought, "I want to be aware of it." Finally, two neighbors reached Imel, warded the dogs off with a steel rod and helped her crawl, bleeding heavily, to safety.

Later that day, the father of the child, a seven-year-old elementary school student named Joshua Pia Perez, would credit Imel with saving his life. "It's like an angel that God sent to protect my son," Cesar Pia told a reporter. "If she wouldn't have been there, perhaps at this time he may be dead."[1] Imel, who needed stitches and surgery and lost one of her eyebrows (but not an eye), received a medal from the sheriff of her county for her valor.

A Perfect Symbol. Kathleen Imel's heroism serves as a perfect symbol of the power we still have, as middle-aged women, to help the next generation. Ironically, some media commentators described Imel as elderly. "I'm only fifty-one," she says, laughing, in an interview. "I have plenty of time left!"

Some commentators, marveling, said that Imel would no doubt be terrified now every time she sees a dog. But her reaction has been the opposite. Walking down the street or passing through a supermarket, her brush with death has left her even more keenly attuned to the cries of children.

For women in search of meaning, Imel serves as a perfect symbol of generativity—the developmental achievement psychologist Erik Erikson described as a central goal at midlife. Generativity is psychologists' dry label for one of our best qualities as human beings: contributing to the welfare of future generations, without expecting a return on that investment. Generativity emerges as central to fulfillment in almost every major psychological theory and long-term study of successful aging. It lends meaning and significance to the goals of each and every archetype in this book, from attaining intimacy to improving the world around us. The behaviors it fosters—caring without strings, respecting the autonomy of youth while generously coaching, mentoring, teaching, parenting, and nurturing them, and working to build a better community—can go far toward satisfying our midlife appetite for meaning.

The importance of generativity can hardly be overemphasized. Two major long-term studies of women, at Radcliffe College and the University of Michigan, found generativity is one of only two factors that actually predict a woman's psychological well-being later in life. The other was the quality of the roles a woman plays at midlife.[2]

William Sadler found in a twelve-year study that generativity is a central part of the personal renaissance some of his subjects experienced at age 50; having attained it, many continued to thrive and grow for the next thirty years.[3] Caring for others,

Sadler found, is more important at midlife and beyond than at any other stage; it is an essential part of any midlife renewal. It is a foundation stone of civilization.

As Imel's example shows, we have at midlife a unique opportunity to practice generativity. We have gained some of the wisdom and skill that comes with age, without yet having lost all of the strength or vitality of youth. In that intersection lies great promise and hope.

A Personal Inspiration. Beyond its symbolic value, Kathleen Imel's heroism has been a personal inspiration to me. A shy and modest woman, she reluctantly consented to an interview. Nothing in her life came easily to Imel, I learned. Raised in a poor family deeply troubled by mental illness, she drifted into a troubled marriage and had two children, then divorced, grew depressed, and dabbled in a risky lifestyle. Her nature was always to reach out and help others—bag ladies at the mall, panhandlers and the like—but the people around her, including her ex-husband, always discouraged her, telling her to "be realistic."

It was a midlife crisis that honed the values Imel displayed on the day of the attack and caused her to redirect her life. The trigger was a diagnosis of schizophrenia in her adult son, the older of her two children, a stunning blow that came in her forties. "Like a slap in the face," the shock led Imel to transform what she describes as a poorly focused and fearful life into a purposeful existence. "I realized I had lived my life either sleepwalking or pleasing everybody else. It transformed me. It was a signal:

Stop hiding the pain of life. Fix what's wrong and do the right thing."

Embracing the Leader archetype, she set aside old fears. For the first time, she trained for a career. Guided by her helping nature, she chose the mental health field, with plans to start her own group foster home for young adults. As a result of the changes she has made, she says, she has learned that "you can believe there is hope for the community. You can walk your talk. Change begins with you."

When her defining moment came on that August day of the dog attack, Imel was trained and ready. Reaching out to help the little boy was so necessary in her mind that she did not even have to think about it. She merely brought forth her inborn desire to help, distilled and refined in the crucible of midlife crisis.

Would that I could provide half as good an example to my children.

Missing the Warning Signs. Some psychologists believe midlife crisis is the result of an "underlying adjustment disorder," that it arises from a psychological inflexibility that is made worse by the challenges of aging.[4]

Guilty as charged. For years, I lived a rigid, one-note example of adulthood. Richly blessed with three wonderful stepchildren, two birth children, and a career I loved, I fell into the trap of trying to do too much. I am happy with the career I built and I loved being a stepparent and a parent. But looking back, I see I hewed for a long time to too confining a self-image. My pose as the perfect wife, worker, and mother was exactly that: a pose, too constraining to be sustained.

Looking back, the extent of my own unconsciousness leaves me breathless. I had tried to lead a responsible life. But unconsciousness is the enemy of integrity; it blinded me to the warning signs of midlife crisis. In my forties, I ignored a mounting emotional numbness. I remember a trip to the beach one weekend with my children, a time that should have been relaxing and filled with joy. I felt only despair.

I also ignored the historical fact of my own mother's rip-roaring midlife crisis.

Repeating History. I was halfway through this book before I realized it was a love letter to my mother.

A loving, devoted parent to whom I was very close, my mother was a wonderful woman. However, I had long believed the life I had set up for myself was entirely different from hers.

She was a stay-at-home mom. I always worked full-time. She married very young, I waited until my late twenties. She looked to my father for leadership in her marriage; I had an egalitarian union. She suffered from low self-esteem; I strived for achievement as an antidote to that affliction.

As the consummate stay-at-home mom, she repressed more venturesome, public parts of herself. As the consummate work-and-family juggler, I repressed more fun-loving, expressive parts of myself.

Mom experienced a raging midlife crisis. Not I, I thought; I would sail serenely across midlife seas that I would force to be placid, damn it.

By her early fifties the vicissitudes of middle age had left my mother with a broken collarbone and a life almost completely transformed. By my early fifties, my midlife turmoil has left me with a broken collarbone and a life almost completely transformed.

The more we change, the more we stay the same. Those who do not learn from history are doomed to repeat it.

A Farm Wife Reborn. I might have learned much from my mother's example. She dropped out of college to marry my father, a farmer, then stayed at home with my brother, sister, and me for years. She and I were as close as a mother and daughter can be, enjoying long, intimate talks. But when Mom volunteered at the family dinner table one day in 1963 that she identified with the women in Betty Friedan's bestseller, *The Feminine Mystique*, that she herself often experienced the "trapped" feeling Friedan described, the room fell silent. Uncomprehending at age 12, I probably looked at her as if she had sprouted two heads.

Health problems touched off a Sonic Boom in my mother's life in her early forties. A severe case of endometriosis nearly killed her before doctors finally performed an emergency hysterectomy. Unaided by hormone therapy, she careened into menopause like a speeding Ferrari hitting a brick wall. In contrast with my own gradual, natural journey across "the Change," my mother's experience with menopause was a dark plunge into the abyss.

The notion of midlife crisis in women wasn't even a puff of smoke on the nation's psychic horizon at that time. Nevertheless, looking back, I can see that my mother found meaning in the Leader archetype. She re-enrolled in college, laboring long into the night on our yellow Formica kitchen table to complete correspondence courses, the snail-mail predecessor of e-learning. She sewed herself beautiful woolen suits and a daring leopard-skin scarf to replace the housedresses of her past. Bucking the mores of our rural community, where middle-class mothers seldom worked for pay, she landed a high school teaching job in English, French, and classical languages and carved out a distinguished decade-long teaching career. The broken collarbone in her case happened in an auto accident during one of her many trips to town; her collarbone, too, remained misshapen for life.

Unfortunately, that life was cut short. My mother would have done more, I am sure, had emphysema not disabled her by her mid-fifties and killed her at age 60. Nevertheless, she achieved at least two of the goals of midlife crisis. She found new meaning in life by picking up a repressed love of literature and weaving it into her life. She filled our farm home with French novels and leather-bound English classics, anchoring her stake in the ground as a scholarly woman.

She also greatly expanded her limits. Her discovery of a passion for French culture gave her so much joy that my father took her to Europe when she was 50—an adventurous journey for a rural American woman of that time. Awakening on their first morning in Paris, my father was alarmed to discover my mother in tears. "Marty, what's wrong?" he asked anxiously.

"I never thought I would see Paris," she said, sobbing. "I am just so happy."

Using Our Thirty-Year Bonus. My mother died so young that I never understood her midlife turbulence in much depth. I moved away and became absorbed in career and marriage. Had I grasped the pattern she set, I might have seen my midlife crisis coming. Instead, I skidded to the breaking point, leaving me too foolish for my years.

Now, conscious at last of what she experienced, I draw inspiration from her example. In her midlife renaissance, she ventured much further beyond the cultural limits of her era than I ever will.

Looking ahead, this generation of women has a unique opportunity to help our daughters do better, and live more fully, for three reasons. First, an unprecedented proportion of us will enjoy what William Sadler calls "the thirty-year life bonus"— nearly three decades of longevity beyond the 50-year milestone.[5] This gives us a lot of years to blaze a generative trail through midlife for our daughters to follow.

Second, middle-aged women today are more likely to experience midlife crises, potentially providing dynamic examples of growth and hope. And third, our children are more likely to still be around home to watch. Today's mothers have driven up the average age at first childbirth by 3.7 years, to 25.1 years in 2002 from 21.4 years in 1970, reflecting their growing tendency to postpone childbearing.[6] Two-fifths of the fifty women in my study still had children living with them when their midlife crises began.

Some of the most moving examples of generativity in my study came from parents wrestling with this overlap of adolescence and middle age. Eleanor, whose story is told in chapter 9, rejected all of her many suitors because she felt they offered nothing to her children. "If they didn't care for my children, I just turned off," she says. "I know that's difficult for men, and I understand that, but nothing else is acceptable." In time, for the sake of her children, "I decided I would just take a pass" on romance. "And that is what I have done." She found satisfaction in developing her screenwriting talent instead.

Others struggled to balance their responsibilities to their children with their responsibilities to themselves. Helena, the artist profiled in chapter 6, worries that her daughters will have trouble paying for college because she has chosen to pursue her art rather than take a high-paying corporate job she would hate. "What's better? Is it better that my daughter sees me fulfilling my dream? I think so."

We can regard this overlap as a curse. The teen years are tough on parents. Marital satisfaction hits its lowest ebb when the first child hits age 14, research shows; single parents face the same stresses.[7] Adding a midlife crisis to the challenges of parenting teens can be a double whammy.

We can also regard it as a blessing. While my midlife crisis gave me more common ground with my two teenagers' hormone-drenched moods than I would have liked, it also led us to many adventures together.

Outing My Inner Outlaw. My midlife crisis erupted in Meltdown at age 49. I was hurting from the death of my father, and from the divorce that had ended my twenty-year marriage. I was missing my three adult stepkids who by then lived thousands of miles away. I was fearful of the looming empty nest I would face in a few years, when my two birth children left home. In the emotionality that is a hallmark of Meltdown, I sank to thoughts of suicide. As Vasalisa learned in the Baltic folktale, there is hell to pay if you let the home fires go out.

In my despair, the value I had long placed upon a stable family life, frugality, career, and exceeding everybody's expectations of me, fell away. A new mantra rang in my mind: "The purpose of life is not to arrive safely at death."

I undertook a frenzied series of snowboarding and camping trips with my kids, sometimes playing hooky from my job to hit the mountain on weekdays after school. While they snowboarded, I skiied beyond the limits of my aging body; adrenaline, I learned, can temporarily erase the pain of arthritis. I took wilderness vacations and bought all-terrain vehicles and a four-wheel-drive SUV to pull them. After a string of calls to my insurance agent to add two ATVs, a trailer, and an SUV to my policy, she began laughing at the sound of my voice on the phone. "What are you adding this time? A Harley?" she'd ask. (I considered that but flunked out of a motorcycle-training class because I could not hold my 500-pound loaner bike upright.)

No question, I needed the insurance. Energized by the "inner teenage boy" Lynn spoke of in chapter 3, I had two bone-crushing crashes flipping ATVs, wrecking a spinal disk in one and my collarbone in another. Contacted by the emergency room physician after my second crash, my longtime doctor's first words over the phone were, "Not again!" Undaunted, I terrified my daughter by laying plans to go bungee-jumping, recanting only because she asked me to do so.

In another Meltdown hallmark, I repeated some mistakes from the past. In my late teens I liked dating rebels and social mavericks for the sense of danger they offered. In midlife, too, my yen for adventure fed my attraction to mavericks and adventurers.

During my only significant relationship, with a rugged outdoorsman with his own love of mischief-making, I nearly threw all my adult duties overboard one Tuesday evening to take off on a Mexican vacation with him. I was sitting in a dank ice rink, watching my son practice with his hockey team, when he called from San Diego on a business trip. Shivering in a sweatshirt and workout pants, I hardly looked like a candidate for an international rendezvous. Yet moments later, I was ready to buy a plane ticket to Mexico for just that purpose.

"Why don't you fly down to Tijuana tomorrow?" My friend's gravelly baritone coming through my cell phone was a lifeline in the damp, drizzly Pacific Northwest night. "We'll head down to Cabo San Lucas for a couple of days. I'm driving a Jag convertible. It's sunny here.

"Meet me at the corner of Second and Revolutionary," he added playfully. I was hooked. The address, in a city I had never seen, conjured up a bacchanalian street scene a world away from my duty-bound life. I had deadlines to meet. Homework to help with. Places to drive my kids, meals to fix, a parent's work to do. I said as much into my cell phone.

"You can figure all that out if you really want to," he said, deftly drawing me out onto the razor's edge. At 51, how many more chances like this would I have? I hung up promising to try.

"Have you lost your mind?" a close friend asked me later that night, after I told her about the invitation and asked her for help covering my home duties.

"I guess I have," I muttered. By the next morning I had settled down. "What was I thinking?" I wondered. Fortunately, I stayed home and tended to business.

But the incident served as a wake-up call: I had some work to do on my life.

Remembering My Lines. A recurring dream came to me during this time, that I was a character in a play—a butterfly, a symbol in dream lore and mythology of the emergent soul.

But I had failed in this dream to memorize my lines. The entire cast and audience around me stopped mid-performance and watched, mystified, as I flopped about the stage in my makeshift wings, scrambling to find my script.

Four years into my midlife crisis, I am slowly remembering my lines. Giving free rein to the Adventurer is merely another path to a one-note life, I have realized. I need to integrate this archetype, not be overpowered by it. I need to strike a delicate balance between restraint and exploration, lest my resurgent midlife desires turn me into a fool.

I spent many weekend days for a while doing farmwork for a friend, who owns a 50-acre pioneer homestead in Oregon's Willamette Valley. Her land lies on the side of a long hill checkered with golden green and brown fields, dotted with spruce and fir. Her horses graze peacefully on its rich grasses. Looking across that land, rolling gracefully down to the banks of a tributary of the Willamette, I understand why it was among the first plots chosen by settlers. It feels like sacred space.

My friend snapped a photo of me whacking weeds there. Wearing thirty-year-old jeans with my hair flying, my skin burned by the August sun and my shoes caked with mud, I look as if I might have just crossed the Rockies by wagon train myself. But working on that land brought me peace, made me feel at home, like the farmwork I did as a child.

Week by week, my friend's hilltop acreage grew greener. Clearing away the tall dead weeds and brush allowed the sun to bring forth the new growth beneath. Tagging along, my kids learned a bit about the farm life I had loved as a child, caring for the horses and the land.

Deepening Relationships. So much healing comes in honoring old remembrances. Recalling how I enjoyed traveling with my parents, I undertook a series of road trips with my kids. My son, daughter, and I enjoy looking for campsites and trying out our ATVs on new trails and dunes.

We enjoy going to what my son calls "our beach house"—a grove of spruce and shore pines a mile off-road in the Oregon Dunes, the 50-mile stretch of rolling sand that graces Oregon's Pacific Coast. Leaving behind the hulking RVs, with their striped awnings and roaring generators squatting on campgrounds of concrete, we deflate our tires, shift into four-wheel drive, and move on into the bush. Hidden there are clearings known only to a few, flat stretches of sand linked by curving beach trails. Amid the beach grass we pitch our tent, camp, and ride ATVs for days.

Nature on the dunes is forgiving, erasing signs of human habitation. Wind scours away imprints of tires, smears of dropped toothpaste and marshmallow, and buries bits of paper and glass. Its cleansing power heals the soul. Here we tote our own firewood and carry our own water. Our family grows closer, our relationships deeper, one by one.

A Hill Too High. Awash in silver sunlight, my son and I sit atop our ATVs at the foot of a giant mountain of sand. All around us are other families on ATVs, madmen in dune buggies and motorcyclists at play, climbing sand hills and chasing each other across the breathtaking expanses of sand.

My son challenges me to a hill climb. Before us sits a 200-yard knoll that looms like the white cliffs of Dover.

"Hit it at three-fourths of full throttle!" my son yells over the din. "And whatever you do, don't stop!" Then he roars away, rides easily up the slope, and spins around at the summit to look down upon me.

I take a deep breath and start my Honda 250 toward the hill at what feels like suicide speed. I gain confidence as my quad roars up the first half of the incline. I must be flying, hitting a breakneck pace. But my engine falters as I near the brow of the hill. I lean forward over the 250's little red fuel tank.

Three men astride powerful dirt bikes, bare biceps shimmering in the sun, roar easily to the summit, stop, and incline their helmeted heads in my direction. Are they marveling at my bravery? No, they are wondering, no doubt, whether I will be forced to do an emergency U-turn or, worse, flip or start rolling backward.

My mouth goes dry. Fear erases thought. What am I to do? My brain offers no clues. On instinct or dumb luck, my foot kicks the gearshift down into first.

The black plastic seat of my quad rises to what feels a nearly vertical slope. Slowing to a crawl, the Honda's engine roars like a 727 as I inch upward. The slope steepens. Whatever you do, don't stop. Whatever you do, don't stop. At last, not breathing, my engine near a stall, I creep over the brow of the hill to a level place and bring the 250 safely to a halt.

Right arm straight overhead, fist clenched in a silent cheer, my son pays tribute. He wheels his quad, spins a cookie, and we roar together over the dunes to the beach. There, with white-caps licking at our wheels and sunlight skittering on surf, we challenge each other, laughing, to a series of drag races. He beats me easily. I am deeply content.

"So," I ask him later, "how'd I do on that hill?"

"Mom, I said three-fourths of full throttle," he says patiently. "You were at one-eighth."

A Little Pie in the Face. As psychotherapist Thomas Moore notes in *Dark Nights of the Soul,* complex and difficult times do not have to be serious. A dark life passage can be "a little like a pie in the face—it relieves you of the stuffy ego you have been wearing," he says. My children have become masters at throwing pies—spotting the contradictions and paradoxes in my behavior and poking fun at them.

On my occasional dates, I revive my teenage love of dancing. My kids collapse with laughter at the thought of Mom cavorting under a disco ball. I am stunned by their insights. Plotting with them one night to make a whimsical family video about cops and robbers, my daughter suggests, "Mom, you can be the outlaw. I think you'd have the most fun that way."

God keeps sending me little jokes, too, jarring incongruities that remind me it is time to weave together the loose ends of my life. Searching for my ATV keys in my purse, I find my osteoporosis medicine instead. Huffing and puffing on the treadmill in my spandex workout duds, I nearly tumble off when my granny-style reading glasses fall to the floor. Laughing with a middle-aged friend about trying to look young, she remarks: "Who cares? Who wants to be Miss December on a Depends calendar anyway?"

Indeed. After buying a new pair of designer sunglasses I think will make me look like Christie Brinkley, I whip them out of my purse, don them with a flourish, and beam a sparkling smile toward my kids.

"Geez, Mom," my son responds, "you look just like Ozzy Osbourne."

A Love Letter to Our Daughters. My children many mornings eat breakfast from a symbol of my mother's midlife crisis: an old aluminum tray, a disk about two and a half feet in diameter hand-stamped with a stencil of a stag and fluted at the edges, of a style popular in the early 1960s. She made it as part of a college course she took to get her bachelor's degree.

I have told my children the story, about how their grandmother, whom they never knew, first did a wonderful job raising her own children, then began a rewarding second career as a teacher. I tell them how she cherished great literature, how she loved learning, how she delighted in her rowdy teenage students.

We stand on our mothers' shoulders, we pass on their legacies, and our own, to our children.

Mindful of Kathleen Imel's example, I strive to pass on to my kids the gift of consciousness. As in her case, midlife crisis has matured and refined my values. In the past, I guided my children toward achievement and status and all the trappings thereof, as promised by the external world. I pressed them to get high grades, I placed them in the most exclusive preschools and schools I could afford, I talked about working hard to enroll at an elite university.

Now, I am working equally hard to get them to set all that aside. More important, I tell them, is living inside-out. Listen to your inner voice and find what you love. Invest your best effort and have a good attitude in all that you undertake, but do not be led astray by the "shoulds" and "ought-to's" of the world. Be guided by your instincts, your passions, by what you love to do, to dream about. Play to your strengths—all your strengths. They will help you set the truest path.

All the while I am silently thinking: Listen to your soul now, so you will not have to start adolescence all over again at 49.

Turning to the Seeker. No words from my study ring more true to me than those of Molly, the California consultant: "One of the main lessons of midlife is that you can't be afraid to be alone with your thoughts."

I am alone more often these days. I bridle at the tightening bonds of aging.

But I am grateful for my adventures. I have faced my fears and found my limits. They lie far beyond what I once imagined. My life is rich beyond measure, and my sights are set on nurturing the future.

I am turning more to the Seeker now. I make a daily discipline of meditation and spiritual studies, trying to learn how to draw closer to God and lead a loving life. In my most peaceful moments, I know this isn't really about me. While I have not found any expressways to nirvana, I believe I am closer to asking the right questions.

How do I balance my responsibility to others with my responsibility to myself?

How can I make my kids' last years at home their best ones?

How can I be of service to others?

How can I learn to savor the moment? It is all I really have.

◆ ◆ ◆

In the wilderness of central Oregon, there is still a mountain I want to climb. Hikers can make the ascent without climbing gear, but it is rough and tall enough to leave a 20-year-old breathless.

There, near the high desert, where the wind scours the land white and tumbleweeds roll with an unending lightness, I know I will be renewed.

Keeping on through midlife, striving for greater growth, is not something we do. It is something we are. I no longer see midlife as a meaningless marathon, but as a vital passage of promise and hope.

In this, I am proof in many ways of the overarching finding of the MacArthur Foundation study: Middle age is often the best time of life.

And that has given me a sizable measure of peace.

Appendix A

✦ ✦ ✦

THE EVOLVING DEFINITION
OF MIDLIFE CRISIS

The concept of midlife crisis has a checkered past. For most of human history, middle age has been seen as a wasteland of decline and decay. Through the middle of the twentieth century, human psychological growth and development was thought to be complete by young adulthood. Life after 40 or 50 was regarded as a time of decline and retirement.

Pioneering psychologist Erik Erikson changed all that in the 1950s by setting forth a powerful theory that human development continues throughout life. People go through eight stages, from infancy through old age, Erikson believed, with each stage building upon the successes of all the previous stages. As discussed in chapter 2, middle adulthood is the important seventh stage that comes along sometime between one's middle twenties and late fifties. Success in middle age, based on Erikson's work, produces a person who derives deep satisfaction from participating in society and contributing to others. Much of life's work is a preparation for midlife, and the later stages are strongly shaped by how well we navigate it.

Decades of subsequent work in psychology were influenced by Erikson's framework of predictable life stages. The term "midlife crisis" was coined in the 1960s by psychologist Elliot Jacques, who found some artists experienced a decline in productivity around age 40. Research psychologist Daniel J. Levinson, a well-known Yale University psychologist and author of *Seasons of a Man's Life*, an influential book on men's stages of development, picked up and used the term in small studies of adult males. He made the term a mainstay of psychological theory when he found many men underwent a time of turbulence as they approached 40. Midlife crisis came to signify a time of loss, self-questioning, and searching that characterized the lives of middle-aged men.

The idea of midlife crisis took deep root in American culture after journalist Gail Sheehy made the term a staple of pop culture. With her bestselling 1976 book *Passages*, Sheehy cast a tractor beam of light into a black hole of public ignorance about adult development. As part of her thoughtful framework of decade-by-decade passages in adult life, she popularized the idea of a midlife crisis as something that strikes most people at or around the age of 40. As her vocabulary entered the vernacular, the public understanding of midlife crisis became oversimplified, as a predictable and universal event.

Many social scientists and psychologists spent a great deal of energy and effort in the 1990s trying to push the pendulum back the other way—to discredit the notion that midlife crisis is a universal experience that occurs at a set time in life. In trying to balance the picture, they challenged not only the universality of midlife crisis, but its very existence.

Today, few social scientists believe all adults pass in lockstep through predictable life stages. Most researchers are embracing a more flexible and diverse view of how adults change and grow through their thirties, forties, and fifties. Each person is seen as developing along an individualized life course at his or her own rate, with turning points cropping up across a wide span of years. Many believe that while we may go through stages, they occur and recur at various times, or even in a different order, based on individual differences. Personality traits that are inborn and shaped very early in life also play a role. Thus adults develop on a path shaped by a combination of personality traits, one's stage of growth, and the social and historical context. The view of midlife crisis I have tried to present in this book is in harmony with this broad definition of adult development.

Jungian psychology has been most helpful to me in mapping a constructive path through midlife. Based on the work of psychoanalyst Carl Jung, people develop a persona, or social facade, in adolescence and early adulthood that provides a way of relating to work, family, and community. As we grow and develop, we strive to make conscious the other parts of ourselves—the traits, needs, desires, and passions—that we have had to suppress for various reasons earlier in life.

This process—becoming an individual and fulfilling one's

capacities and potential—is called individuation, and midlife crisis can be regarded as a time of rapid progress on this path. The goal is to integrate all the parts of our personalities into a revitalized, fuller, richer self. This process brings with it the potential for deep psychological healing. The energies we bring to these tasks "cannot be contained, nor can the soul at midlife," psychoanalyst Murray Stein writes. As revealed in the stories of the women in this book, they drive us forward, toward wholeness, with an energy that can transform.

Appendix B

✦ ✦ ✦

THE FIFTY-WOMAN STUDY

The nonrandom study upon which this book is largely based was conducted between December 2003 and August 2004. The fifty subjects were selected based on their own assent that they had experienced "a turbulent midlife transition" at some time between the ages of 38 and 55.

The women were identified through e-mails I received in my work as a columnist; networking with news sources, professional contacts, and friends; and newspaper advertisements in the *New York Times* and *Chicago Tribune*. I interviewed each woman in depth about her childhood, career, family, midlife experience, and the outcome of her midlife transition. The interviews lasted from one to six hours, based on each woman's speaking style and preference. All were offered confidentiality to allow them to speak freely.

The sample encompasses most of the United States, with one woman from Canada. The largest group, sixteen of the women, live in the Northeast, including New York, Pennsylvania, Connecticut, New Jersey, and Washington, D.C. Three live in New England, all in Massachusetts.

The second largest group, twelve women, came from the western states of California and Oregon. The Midwest produced eight subjects, from Michigan, Missouri, Illinois, and Minnesota. Six came from the southeastern states of Tennessee, Florida, Louisiana, Georgia, and Alabama. The rest were from the Mountain states, the Southwest, or Toronto, Canada.

I made an effort to include women from a wide range of occupations and income levels. The largest group, nine of the women, were in corporate management jobs, ranging from CEOs to low-ranking middle managers. Eight were professionals, including lawyers or audiologists. Six were writers or artists, including actors. Five of the women owned and ran their own companies. Another five were teachers or counselors. Four had administrative jobs, including such posts as billing administrator or staff assistant. Four worked in health care or human services. Four were at-home mothers with children still at home. Four worked as independent consultants or freelancers. One was retired from a corporate management job.

Sixty percent of the women were married at the time of the interviews. Fifteen were divorced, three had never been married, and two were separated from their husbands. Twenty of the women had children still living at home, nineteen had grown children, and eleven had no children at all.

Appendix C

✦ ✦ ✦

THE ARCHETYPES AND
RESEARCH ON AGING

Each of the archetypes that emerged from my study of female midlife crisis is tied to qualities and capabilities that contribute to health, happiness, and well-being in old age.

That conclusion is based upon four major studies. The first, the so-called Nun Study, was a long-term look at why 678 Catholic sisters, ranging in age from 74 to 106, lived so long. Conducted by David Snowdon, an epidemiologist by training and one of the world's leading experts on Alzheimer's disease, the study identified the practices and attitudes among the nuns that were linked to better mental functioning, better health, and fewer disabilities. Snowdon summarized his findings in *Aging with Grace: What the Nun Study Teaches Us About Leading Longer, Healthier, and More Meaningful Lives* (Bantam Books, 2001).

A second study, the "Harvard Study of Adult Development," is a fifty-year examination of 824 people from adolescence throughout their lives. Headed by Harvard Medical School psychiatrist and researcher George Vaillant, the study offers models that show how and why old people end up happy—or not. Vaillant summarized his findings in *Aging Well: Surprising Guideposts to a Happier Life* (Little, Brown, 2002).

Separate from the "Midlife in the United States" project, a third research project, the MacArthur Foundation "Study of Successful Aging," is a highly focused set of studies conducted between 1984 and 1995 by an interdisciplinary team of top scientists. It examines the role of a wide range of factors, from diet and exercise to lifestyle and attitude, in shaping longevity and well-being in old age. The findings are summarized in *Successful Aging* by John W. Rowe and Robert L. Kahn (Dell, 1998).

A final work, a twelve-year study of several dozen men and women between the ages of 45 and 80 by sociology professor William A. Sadler, identifies six principles of growth and renewal after forty. He describes his research in *The Third Age: Six Principles for Growth and Renewal after 40* (Perseus Publishing, 2000). While this work lacks the scholarly comprehensiveness of the other three studies, it is unusually clear and concise in its focus on midlife growth and renewal.

The following table marks the linkages between selected traits and competencies found to be important by these researchers and the traits and competencies linked to the archetypes described in this book. My hope is that this table will clarify the powerful relationship between successfully integrating the six archetypes of midlife crisis and maximizing one's prospects of a healthy, happy old age.

Relating the Archetype to a Healthy Old Age

NAME OF ARCHETYPE*

Traits/Competencies	Lover	Leader	Adventurer	Artist	Gardener	Seeker
The Nun Study						
Positive emotion†	x	x	x	x	x	x
The MacArthur Study						
Education		x				x
Physical fitness			x			
High self-esteem	x	x	x	x	x	x
The Harvard Study						
Openness to new ideas		x	x	x		x
Caring about others	x				x	x
Enjoyment of past accomplishments					x	
Hope	x	x	x	x	x	x
Autonomy and initiative		x	x	x	x	x
Capacity for joy and play			x	x	x	
Making and keeping friends			x		x	
The Sadler Study						
Risk-taking ability	x	x	x	x		
Realistic optimism	x	x	x	x	x	x
Positive midlife identity	x	x	x	x	x	x
Deepening relationships	x				x	
More meaningful work		x		x		
More play			x	x		
Caring for self	x	x	x	x	x	x
Caring for others	x	x			x	x
Caring for the earth					x	

*While all of these qualities may be present to some degree in each archetype, the linkages are based on a particular tendency to bring forth the trait or attribute in someone in whom it had been latent.
†"Positive emotion" in this context means optimistic or upbeat expressions as gauged in autobiographies written by the nuns as novices.

Notes

✦ ✦ ✦

Introduction

1. Murray Stein, *In Midlife: A Jungian Perspective* (Dallas, Tex.: Spring Publications, 1983), p. 121. The Jungian concepts cited in this book are owed largely to Dr. Stein.

1: Midlife Crisis: Not Just for Men Anymore

1. Elaine Wethington, "Expecting Stress: Americans and the 'Midlife Crisis,'" *Motivation and Emotion* 24 (2000): 85–103.

2. National Center for Education Statistics, "Post-secondary Institutions in the United States: Fall 2002," and "Degrees and Other Awards Conferred, 2001–2002," NCES #2004-154, Washington, D.C., October 2003, p. 5.

3. Deborah Carr, "Psychological Well-Being across Three Cohorts," in *How Healthy Are We? A National Study of Well-Being at Midlife*, ed. Orville G. Brim, Carol D. Ryff, and Ronald C. Kessler (Chicago: University of Chicago Press, 2004), p. 477.

4. James T. Bond, Cynthia Thompson, Ellen Galinsky, and David Prottas, "Highlights: National Study of the Changing Workforce" (New York: Families and Work Institute, 2003), p. 23.

5. Lydia Saad, Jim Harter, and Larry Emond, original data run from Gallup poll, Gallup Organization, Princeton, N.J., March 2004. Based on the 2001–2003 Lifestyle GPSS Aggregate, transmitted March 29, 2004, e-mail memorandum.

6. Ann Clurman, original data analysis from Yankelovich Monitor, Chapel Hill, N.C., transmitted May 17, 2004, e-mail memorandum.

7. Robert Prisuta and Sarah Zapolsky, "Baby Boomers Envision Retirement II," AARP and Roper ASW, Washington, D.C., 2004, p. 53. Information supplemented by author's telephone interview with R. Prisuta.

8. Alice Rossi, unpublished memorandum to colleagues in the "Midlife in the United States" study, Amherst, Mass., February 14, 1998, p. 5.

9. Edward O. Laumann, University of Chicago, telephone interview with author, April 22, 2004.

10. Xenia P. Montenegro, "Lifestyles, Dating and Romance: A Study of Midlife Singles," AARP and Knowledge Networks Inc., Washington, D.C., September 2003, p. 8.

11. Tom Smith, National Opinion Research Center, Chicago, July 23, 2004, e-mail memorandum.

12. Michael W. Wiederman, "Extramarital Sex: Prevalence and Correlates in a National Survey," *Journal of Sex Research* 34 (1997): 167–74.

13. Steven P. Martin, University of Maryland, original analysis of 2001 Survey of Income and Program Participation data, U.S. Bureau of the Census, March 26, 2004, e-mail memorandum.

14. Xenia P. Montenegro, "The Divorce Experience: A Study of Divorce at Midlife and Beyond," AARP and Knowledge Networks, Washington, D.C., May 2004.

15. Martin, e-mail memorandum.

16. Janet Lever, University of California, Los Angeles, March 18, 2004, e-mail memorandum based on *Elle* magazine and MSNBC.com, "Office Sex & Romance Survey," 2002.

17. National Center for Educational Statistics, Table 174.

18. DDB Life Style Study, "Religion in Middle Age," original data analysis, Chicago, September 16, 2004.

19. Matt Schueller, Leisure Trends Group, "Middle-Aged Women and Leisure Activities," original study, Boulder, Colorado, September 14, 2004.

20. Harvey Lauer, "IHRSA/ASD Health Club Trend Report (1987–2002)," and "The Superstudy of Sports Participation," *Fitness Activities* vol. 1 (Hartsdale, N.Y.: American Sports Data Inc., 2002).

21. C. V. Wiseman, S. R. Sunday, F. Klapper, W. Harrison, and K. A. Halmi, "Changing Patterns of Hospitalization in Eating Disorder Patients," *International Journal of Eating Disorders* 30 (2001): 69–74.

22. Edward Cumella, Remuda Ranch, Wickenburg, Arizona, May 12, 2004, e-mail memorandum.

23. Alice Rossi, "The Menopausal Transition and Aging Processes," in *How Healthy Are We?* ed. Brim et al., pp. 189–90.

24. Saad et al., Gallup poll, 2004.

25. Ravenna Helson, Mills Longitudinal Study, University of California, Berkeley, March 28, 2004, e-mail memorandum.

26. Pauline Maki, University of Illinois at Chicago, Center for Cognitive Medicine, August 24, 2004, e-mail memorandum.

27. Nancy E. Avis and Sonja M. McKinlay, "The Massachusetts Women's Health Study: An Epidemiologic Investigation of the Menopause," *Journal of the American Medical Women's Association* 50 (March/April 1995).

28. Rehabilitation Institute of Chicago, "2004 Survey of Baby Boomers."

29. Prisuta and Zapolsky, "Baby Boomers Envision Retirement," Table 129.

30. Elaine Wethington, Ronald C. Kessler, and Joy E. Pixley, "Turning Points in Adulthood," in *How Healthy Are We?* ed. Brim et al., pp. 600–8.

31. Elaine Wethington, telephone interview with author, August 10, 2003.

32. Phyllis Moen and Elaine Wethington, "Midlife Development in a Life Course Context," in *Life in the Middle: Psychological and Social Development in Middle Age*, ed. S. L. Willis and J. D. Reid (San Diego: Academic Press, 1999), pp. 3–24.

33. Clurman, Yankelovich Monitor.

2: *The Breaking Point: Why Midlife Crisis Has So Much Power*

Note: The epigraph is from Mary E. Mebane, *Mary, Wayfarer: An Autobiography* (New York: Viking Press, 1983), p. 42.

1. Murray Stein, *In Midlife: A Jungian Perspective* (Dallas, Tex.: Spring Publications, 1983), p. 78.

2. Clarissa Pinkola Estes, *Women Who Run with the Wolves* (New York: Ballantine Books, 1995), p. 93.

3. Stein, "In Midlife," p. 93.

4. Dany Levy, "On Language: Chickspeak," *The New York Times Magazine*, August 22, 2004, 18.

5. Stein, *In Midlife*, pp. 95–100.

6. Ibid., pp. 83–105.

7. Gene D. Cohen, *The Creative Age: Awakening Human Potential in the Second Half of Life* (New York: Quill, 2001), pp. 50–52.

8. Gene D. Cohen, telephone interview with author, October 15, 2004.

9. R. C. Kessler, K. A. McGonagle, M. Swartz, et al., "Sex and Depression in the National Comorbidity Survey. I: Lifetime Prevalence, Chronicity and Recurrence," *Journal of Affective Disorders* 29 (October–November 1993): 85–96.

10. Carol Magai and Beth Halpern, "Emotional Development During the Middle Years," in *Handbook of Midlife Development*, ed. Margie E. Lachman (New York: John Wiley & Sons, 2001), pp. 333–34.

11. E. A. Vandewater, J. M. Ostrove, and A. J. Stewart, "Predicting Women's Well-Being in Midlife: The Importance of Personality Development and Social Role Involvements," *Journal of Personality and Social Personality* 72 (1997): 1147–60.

12. Jutta Heckhausen, "Adaptation and Resilience in Midlife," in *Handbook of Midlife Development*, ed. Lachman, pp. 354–55.

3: *The Adventurer*

1. Robyn Savage, Mountain Travel Sobek, Emeryville, Calif., August 23, 2004, e-mail memorandum.

2. David Zubick, Racing Adventures, Scottsdale, Ariz., August 18, 2004, e-mail memorandum.

3. Paul Huddle, Multisports.com, Encinitas, Calif., August 23, 2004, e-mail memorandum.

4. George Vaillant, *Aging Well: Surprising Guideposts to a Happier Life* (New York: Little, Brown, 2002), p. 224.

5. Ibid., pp. 235–36.

6. Alice Rossi, "The Menopausal Transition and Aging Processes," in *How Healthy Are We? A National Study of Well-Being at Midlife*, ed. Orville G. Brim et al. (Chicago: University of Chicago Press, 2004), pp. 179–89.

4: The Lover

1. William A. Sadler, *The Third Age: Six Principles for Growth and Renewal After 40* (Cambridge, Mass.: Perseus Publishing, 2000), p. 147.

2. Alice Rossi, "The Menopausal Transition and Aging Processes," in *How Healthy Are We? A National Study of Well-Being at Midlife*, ed. Orville G. Brim et al. (Chicago: University of Chicago Press, 2004), pp. 189–90.

3. Constance Swank, Linda Fisher, and Robert Prisuta, "AARP/ Modern Maturity Sexuality Study," AARP and NFO Research, Inc., Washington, D.C., August 3, 1999, pp. 24–27.

4. Thomasina H. Sharpe, "Adult Sexuality," *Family Journal: Counseling and Therapy for Couples and Families* 11 (October 2003): 423.

5. Ibid., 420–26.

5: The Leader

1. George Vaillant, *Aging Well: Surprising Guideposts to a Happier Life* (New York: Little, Brown, 2002), p. 311.

2. Dan P. McAdams, "Generativity at Midlife," in *Handbook of Midlife Development*, ed. Margie E. Lachman (New York: John Wiley & Sons, 2001), pp. 412, 419.

3. L. K. Cartwright and P. Wink, "Personality Change in Women Physicians from Medical Student Years to Mid-40s," *Psychology of Women Quarterly* 18 (1994): 291–308.

4. Hedy Ratner, Women's Business Development Center, Chicago, August 10, 2004, e-mail memorandum.

5. Myra Hart, Professor of Management, Harvard Business School, August 11, 2004, e-mail memorandum.

6. D. Carr, "The Fulfillment of Career Dreams at Midlife: Does It Matter for Women's Mental Health?" *Journal of Health and Social Behavior* 38 (1992): 331–44.

6: The Artist

1. R. Maduro, "Artistic Creativity and Aging in India," *International Journal of Aging and Human Development* 5 (1974): 303–29.

2. George Vaillant, *Aging Well: Surprising Guideposts to a Happier Life* (New York: Little, Brown, 2002), p. 13.

3. Robert J. Sternberg, Elena L. Grigorenko, and Stella Oh, "The Development of Intelligence at Midlife," in *Handbook of Midlife Development*, ed. Margie E. Lachman (New York: John Wiley & Sons, 2001), pp. 238–39.

4. Gene D. Cohen, *The Creative Age: Awakening Human Potential in the Second Half of Life* (New York: Quill, 2001), pp. 50–52, and October 15, 2004, telephone interview.

5. Margie E. Lachman and Jacquelyn Boone James, "Charting the Course of Midlife Development: An Overview," in *Multiple Paths of Midlife Development*, ed. Margie E. Lachman and Jacquelyn Boone James (Chicago: University of Chicago Press, 1997), p. 7.

6. Mona Lisa Schulz, September 2, 2004, e-mail memorandum.

7: The Gardener

Note: Epigraph from Henry D. Thoreau, *The Journal of Henry D. Thoreau*, ed. Bradford Torry and Francis H. Allen (New York: Dover Publications, 1962).

1. George Vaillant, *Aging Well: Surprising Guideposts to a Happier Life* (New York: Little, Brown, 2002), pp. 308–10.

2. Constance Swank, Linda Fisher, and Robert Prisuta, "AARP/Modern Maturity Sexuality Study," AARP and NFO Research, Inc., Washington, D.C., August 3, 1999, p. 24.

3. Simmons School of Management, Center for Gender in Organizations, "2003 Leadership Conference Survey Results," Boston.

4. William Fleeson, "The Quality of American Life at the End of the Century," in *How Healthy Are We? A National Study of Well-Being at Midlife*, ed. Orville G. Brim et al. (Chicago: University of Chicago Press, 2004), pp. 257–62.

5. Deborah Carr, "Psychological Well-Being across Three Cohorts: A Response to Shifting Work-Family Opportunities and Expectations?" in *How Healthy Are We?* pp. 461–79.

8: The Seeker

1. Alice S. Rossi, "Social Responsibility to Family and Community," in *How Healthy Are We? A National Study of Well-Being at Midlife*, ed. Orville G. Brim et al. (Chicago: University of Chicago Press, 2004), pp. 569–71.

2. Lydia Saad, Gallup poll, original study by the Gallup Organization, Princeton, N.J., September 22, 2004, e-mail memorandum.

3. DDB Life Style Survey, DDB Worldwide, Chicago, original analysis of longitudinal data, September 16, 2004 memorandum.

4. Constance Swank, Linda Fisher, and Robert Prisuta, "AARP/Modern Maturity Sexuality Study," AARP and NFO Research, Inc., Washington, D.C., August 3, 1999, p. 24.

5. Jeff Levin and Robert Joseph Taylor, "Age Differences in Patterns and Correlates of the Frequency of Prayer," *The Gerontologist* 37 (1997): 75–88.

6. C. D. Ryff, B. H. Singer, and K. A. Palmersheim, "Social Inequalities in Health and Well-Being: The Role of Relational and Religious Protective Factors," in *How Healthy Are We? A National Study of Well-Being at Midlife*, ed. Orville G. Brim et al. (Chicago: University of Chicago Press, 2004), pp. 110–12.

7. Jeff Levin, "Religion," In *The Encyclopedia of Aging*, 4th edition (New York: Springer Publishing Co.), in press.

8. Jeff Levin, "Age Differences in Mystical Experience," *The Gerontologist* 33 (1993): 507–13.

9. Jeff Levin, September 13, 2004, e-mail memorandum.

10. T. W. Smith and S. Kim, "The Vanishing Protestant Majority," in GSS Social Change Report no. 49, National Opinion Research Center, University of Chicago, July 2004, p. 14.

11. Carl Jung, "Psychotherapists or the Clergy," in *Modern Man in Search of a Soul* (New York: Harvest Books, 1955).

12. Smith and Kim, "Vanishing Protestant Majority," p. 14.

9: Sharing Our Wisdom

1. T. C. Antonucci, H. Akiyama, and A. Merline, "Dynamics of Social Relationships at Midlife," in *Handbook of Midlife Development*, ed. Margie E. Lachman (New York: John Wiley & Sons, 2001), p. 589.

10: Across the Generations

1. Holly Danks, "Father Says 'Angel' Saved Son during Dogs' Attack," *The Oregonian*, July 28, 2004.

2. Dan P. McAdams, "Generativity in Midlife," in *Handbook of Midlife Development*, ed. Margie E. Lachman (New York: John Wiley & Sons, 2001), p. 425.

3. William A. Sadler, *The Third Age: Six Principles for Growth and Renewal after 40* (Cambridge, Mass.: Perseus Publishing, 2000), pp. 14–15, 150–52.

4. Thomasina H. Sharpe, "Adult Sexuality," *Family Journal: Counseling and Therapy for Couples and Families* 11 (October 2003): 424.

5. Sadler, *The Third Age*, pp. 1–21.

6. Centers for Disease Control, National Center for Health Statistics, "Births: Final Data for 2002," *National Vital Statistics Reports* 52, no. 10 (December 17, 2003): 6.

7. J. M. Gottman and R. W. Levenson, "The Timing of Divorce: Predicting When a Couple Will Divorce over a 14-Year Period," *Journal of Marriage and the Family* 62 (August 2000): 737–45.

Bibliography

✦ ✦ ✦

Anderson, Joan. *A Year by the Sea: Thoughts of an Unfinished Woman*. New York: Broadway Books, 2000. A loving wife and supportive mother plunges into midlife crisis, fleeing an empty nest and a stagnant marriage for an oceanside cottage where new possibilities unfold.

Bridges, William. *Transitions: Making Sense of Life's Changes*. 2nd ed. Cambridge, Mass.: Da Capo Press, 2004. A classic template for understanding the ebb and flow of adult life, showing how predictable stages of loss, emptiness, and renewal mark each new phase.

Bronson, Po. *What Should I Do with My Life? The True Story of People Who Answered the Ultimate Question*. New York: Random House, 2002. Well-told stories of fifty people who changed the course of their lives midstream, providing valuable templates for overcoming missteps and making bold changes.

Cohen, Gene D. *The Creative Age: Awakening Human Potential in the Second Half of Life*. New York: Quill, 2001. A vibrant and informative guide to sustaining creativity while aging, including its importance to our health, mental vitality, and well-being.

Hetherington E. Mavis, and John Kelly. *For Better or Worse: Divorce Reconsidered*. New York: W. W. Norton, 2002. For those whose midlife turmoil threatens a marriage, this hard-headed look at the after-effects of divorce, based on a landmark thirty-year study, will help evaluate the risks.

Jamison, Kay Redfield. *Exuberance: The Passion for Life.* New York: Alfred A. Knopf, 2004. An exploration of one of life's most uplifting emotions and how it fuels our most creative achievements, from music and religion to laughter and play.

Kreinin, Tamara, and Barbara Camens. *Girls' Night Out: Celebrating Women's Groups across America.* New York: Crown Publishers, 2002. A lively and inspiring portrait of fifteen diverse women's groups, with guidance on how to form one.

Langer, J. Ellen. *Mindfulness.* Reading, Mass.: Addison-Wesley, 1989. A landmark book on the art of being mentally present and fully conscious in various realms of life, including the beneficial effects of mindfulness on the aging process.

LeShan, Lawrence. *How to Meditate: A Guide to Self-Discovery.* New York: Little, Brown, 1974. A simple, straightforward guide to meditation, including an explanation of how and why it can open doors to ethical and psychological growth.

Lindbergh, Anne Morrow. *Gift from the Sea.* New York: Pantheon Books, 1975. A brief, lyrical classic that explores with poetic grace many of the same themes women seek to understand today, including simplicity, solitude, and purposeful living.

Moore, Thomas. *Care of the Soul.* New York: Gotham Books, 2004. A deep and thoughtful look at how life's darkest and most difficult times can heal and invigorate the spirit and reawaken creative potential.

Sewell, Marilyn, ed. *Breaking Free: Women of Spirit at Midlife and Beyond.* Boston: Beacon Press, 2004. A collection of vivid, often poetic essays by notable women on a variety of experiences at midlife, from swimming icy Montana rivers at age 60 to launching a difficult teenage boy.

Stein, Murray. *In Midlife: A Jungian Perspective.* Dallas: Spring Publications, 1983. A scholarly analysis of the transformative power of midlife upheaval, including rich discussion of dreams, archetypes, and individuals' stories.

Trafford, Abigail. *Crazy Time: Surviving Divorce and Building a New Life.* Rev. ed. New York: HarperPerennial, 1992. This updated version of a 1982 bestseller, the first book to deal honestly with the psychological aftermath of divorce, offers a clear, nonideological road map through divorce recovery.

Weiner-Davis, Michele. *Divorce Busting*. New York: Fireside, 1992. A tough-minded advice book with the explicit goal of helping troubled couples patch up their ailing marriages.

Acknowledgments

✦ ✦ ✦

I am grateful to so many people for helping and supporting this work. My column in the "Personal Journal" section of *The Wall Street Journal* was the starting point, and I am in debt in the most fundamental sense to executives and editors at the newspaper, particularly Paul Steiger, Joanne Lipman, and Edward Felsenthal, for creating the editorial context and allowing me the intellectual freedom to try new ideas and take varied approaches in writing and reporting. To my editor, Stefanie Ilgenfritz, I owe thanks for her curiosity and good questions, which gave rise to the column idea. To my readers, I owe gratitude for their wonderful stories and for their generosity, insight, and humor in sharing them.

I am deeply indebted to my agent, Amanda Urban, for the idea for this book, for help in its early-stage development, and for the encouragement to execute it. My editor at Holt, Jennifer Barth, provided both inspiration and a wealth of insightful suggestions, masterfully timed, that enabled me to develop my ideas more fully. I am grateful to Jennifer, not only for her superb editing of the manuscript but for her patience as I worked to complete it.

The research for this book was enriched by the generous contributions of hundreds of people. In particular, I want to thank Larry Emond and colleagues at the Gallup Organization; Ann Clurman and Margaret Gardner at Yankelovich Partners; Matt Schueller and his colleagues at Leisure Trends; Dave Howell at National Election Studies; Jim Crimmins at the DDB Life Style Survey; Robert Prisuta and his colleagues at AARP; Elaine Wethington at Cornell University; Janet Lever at the University of California at Los Angeles; Thomasina Sharpe at the University of South Alabama; Steve Martin at the University of Maryland, College Park; Alice S. Rossi at the University of Massachusetts; Ravenna Helson at the University of California at Berkeley; and Bert Brim and Carol Ryff at the MacArthur Foundation's Research Network on Successful Midlife Development.

To the fifty women who so generously and wholeheartedly shared their life stories for this book, I owe the lion's share of whatever wisdom and richness may be found here. I am grateful to Dr. Murray Stein and Dr. Jan O. Stein for my early training in Jungian theory and for their inspired guidance in how it manifests in our lives.

And to my birth children, Cristin and James, I owe gratitude for their patience and understanding as I worked long hours on this project. My hope is that this book in some small way will return that gift, by enabling them to lead richer, fuller lives.

About the Author

SUE SHELLENBARGER is the creator and writer of the *Wall Street Journal*'s "Work & Family" column. The former chief of the *Journal*'s Chicago news bureau, Shellenbarger started the column in 1991 to provide the nation's first regular coverage of the growing conflict between work and family and its implications for the workplace and society.

Questions for Discussion

1. Joseph Campbell said: "Midlife is when you reach the top of the ladder and find that it was against the wrong wall." Give examples of how this might pertain to your own life.

2. Female midlife crisis is not necessarily brought on by the fear of death (which is more common in men), but by major life transitions or events. Evidence suggests that women go through bigger upheavals than men but deal with midlife turbulence better, why?

3. Why is there more potential for crisis for women who are successful? Why do some women continue smoothly through middle life, and others experience complete upheavals?

4. How can the fear of losing your ability to attract men and to be thought of as attractive facilitate a crisis?

5. Compare the cultural effects of baby boom women's midlife crises to their predecessors in the 60s and 70s.

6. Discuss which one of the archetypes best fits your personality. (Adventurer, Lover, Leader, Artist, Gardener, Seeker.)

7. "Growth hurts," says a Cornell University researcher. Discuss ways to deal with the surprise of pain at such a mature stage of life.

8. Which mode of midlife crisis describes your experience and why: Sonic Boom, Moderate, Slow Burn, Flameout, Meltdown, Non-Starter.

9. How does making a choice for yourself make others in your life happier? How can you tell whether the risks involved in shaking up your life are worth the outcome? Is it necessary to take a leap of faith to push yourself through a midlife crisis?

10. Discuss ways in which the archetype of the Seeker can help women reconnect to themselves and to the things that have meaning in their lives.

11. One of the main lessons of midlife crisis is that you cannot be afraid to be alone, or alone with your thoughts. How can you rebuild a relationship with yourself? What are some of the things you can learn from midlife crisis?

12. How can women avoid the isolation that many feel at this stage of life? What are some of the ways in which women can share their stories and experiences to help themselves and others?

Start your own Second Act Sisterhood

One of the toughest aspects of a midlife crisis for most women is the isolation they feel. Our culture affords no customary, established ways for midlife women to meet, share their experiences, and find a sounding board for the dreams and questions that surface for many of us at midlife. Yet a critical difference between women who manage a midlife transition successfully and those who remain non-starters is often a supportive network of female friends who offer feedback and encouragement. If you read *The Breaking Point* to better understand your own restlessness or frustration, you may want to consider starting a Second Act Sisterhood (SAS). Here are some recommendations:

1. Gather a group of friends who are also in the middle of life, however you want to define it, and who have some goal or dream or desire they would like to pursue, no matter how distant or difficult it may seem. This might be either a new or existing group, such as a book or investment club that wishes to shift gears for a while. The meeting should be held in a place where everyone will feel at ease—perhaps at a restaurant or in a participant's home.

2. Have each person discuss her dream along with the fears and obstacles that stand in her way. It may be helpful to assign each woman a defined period of time to speak and hear feedback, such as fifteen to thirty minutes each.

3. After each woman has presented her goal or desire, the other women should each be allowed time to respond. Only positive feedback or support is permitted; disapproval, criticism, and sarcasm are not allowed. Even if someone's ambition seems far fetched, the members of the group should support the member's wish for change and brainstorm for tactics and ideas that could make it happen.

4. Members should lend more than vocal support to each other if they can. For example, if one group member wants to pursue outdoor activities and adventure and another is a member of a ski club, this is an ideal opportunity for one member to help another realize her ambition.

5. Set a regular meeting time when members can reconvene and talk about progressing toward their dream, perhaps bi-weekly, monthly, or quarterly, either indefinitely or for an agreed-upon period, to share and support each other's midlife dreams, goals, and renewal.

6. Every meeting should offer each woman an opportunity to present her experiences and steps forward. Every Second Act Sisterhood member should know that her voice is heard and that she is in good company as she continues on her pathway toward personal growth.

One of the women profiled in *The Breaking Point* said that hearing other women's stories of midlife crisis and resolution is like passing a recipe on to someone else. With your Second Act Sisterhood you're ensuring that one person's recipe for change and happiness can be shared, adapted, and applied by other women living through a similar transition.